WINNING

POLITICAL

DEBATES

RANDY EVANS
&
MICHAEL HESTER

BOLD COLORS
PUBLISHING

Printed in the United States of America

ISBN: 978-1735718002 (Paperback)
ISBN: 978-1735718019 (Hardcover)

Library of Congress Control Number: 2020917358

email us at:
winningpoliticaldebates@gmail.com

or visit our website:
www.WinningPoliticalDebates.com
for more information

BOLD COLORS
PUBLISHING

DEDICATION

This book is dedicated to the memory and legacy of Dr. Chester Gibson, whose love of debate was surpassed only by the love for his family. His career in forensics spanned four decades, which included coaching champions at both the high school and collegiate levels, as well as hosting multiple state and national championship tournaments. As a scholar of communication and coach of argumentation, Dr. Gibson had an unsurpassed passion for debate. His dedication to promoting critical thinking and rhetorical skills in the lives of his students played a vital role in the personal and professional development of thousands of individuals, including each of this book's contributors.

ACKNOWLEDGMENTS

Acknowledging all those who made this book possible would be an impossible task since it is the culmination of a lifetime of learning from high school forward. Needless to say, the primary motivator for transitioning from arguing to debating to winning was Dr. Chester Gibson.

Back in 1976 when Speaker Gingrich was losing his second bid for Congress and I was just starting at West Georgia College, Dr. Gibson had already moved the small rural college light-years in intercollegiate debate. In 1978, Speaker Gingrich won his Congressional election, and my debate partner Paul Weathington and I were among the best debate teams in the country.

From there, big things happened for all of us. But none of us ever forgot the root of the discipline, focus, and training we received. It was the foundation for many other big things to come.

Yet, it would be unfair to omit the assistant debate coaches, John Wittig and Walter Ulrich, who helped mightily along the way. Each, in their own way, refined some rough spots, mentored some soft spots, and otherwise reinforced what Dr. Gibson instilled in his debaters—the skill to win.

As a whole, the West Georgia debate program has produced some incredible leaders. Indeed, the names on the trophies are a testament to the accomplishments of those trained in a program focused on winning. Debating for the sake of debating was never enough. The goal was to win.

Unfortunately, like any accomplished competitor, winning takes a lot more than skill and determination. It takes time and focus. Inevitably, this is time and focus diverted from those we love most.

So, this book would not be possible without the forgiving patience of those who paid that price, including especially my wife Linda. This book did not write itself. Instead, the hours and attention came from her and, hence, she has contributed much to its creation and publication.

Many others including alumni of the West Georgia debate program have also devoted time, energy, and talent to this undertaking. It would be impossible to list them all, but it is all of them together that made it possible.

And, of course, it was Speaker Gingrich who took a struggling debater to Washington, D.C., to give him a chance and then let me ride along contributing where I could as he did the unimaginable. As he did, another history professor, Dr. Mel Steely, coached, mentored, and pushed things along in a way that only he could do.

Meanwhile, Kathy Lubbers has proven yet again that she is the secret ingredient for making lemonade out of lemons. It is a skill set that is often envied but rarely replicated.

Finally, Mike Hester undertook the Herculean effort of taking raw material and making it into a meaningful, understandable, and usable book. He applied the models developed by Dr. Gibson and refined over the years to produce for everyone of every persuasion a toolkit for winning at political debate. Special thanks to Duane Theobald for providing a set of expert eyes for the final proofing.

If the meaningful exchange of ideas is the cornerstone of a free and evolving civil society, Dr. Chester Gibson has done his part for a generation of debaters inspired by one loving debate coach. Hopefully, future debaters will find some part of the techniques contained in this book will help them "win the political debate" of their times.

— Randy Evans

Acknowledgement of those whose efforts made this book possible must start with its primary author, Randy Evans, who has generously translated his political expertise into support of UWG Debate. As a fellow graduate of Northside High School and West Georgia College, his success continues to inspire me. During my collaboration on this book, I was fortunate to work with Kathy Lubbers, whose brilliance and patience with me have been invaluable blessings. Finally, special thanks to the following for their assistance and support: Nikki Adair, Lashara Barnes, Faye Gibson, Nathan Holmes, Cary Ichter, Shawn Isaacs, Patty Jiles, Anita Lamar, Geoff and Sarah Lundeen, Lacressa Morrow, Bruce Rogers, James Sizemore, Daniel Turner, Kevin and Holly Wangerin, and Paul Weathington.

— Michael Hester

TABLE OF CONTENTS

FOREWORD

Newt Gingrich, former Speaker of the
U.S. House of Representatives

I am delighted to write this preface to Randy Evans' important book on the principles of successful debating.

I have known Randy since 1976. He was a brilliant college debater, a national level debater coached by the legendary Chester Gibson at West Georgia College. Coach Gibson had a remarkable record of teaching young people a disciplined system of careful preparation and the application of principles in the debate itself.

In fact, many of Gibson's students, from what was then a small Georgia state college, found themselves winning in tournaments against Ivy League debaters with great pedigrees but less effective training.

It was Coach Gibson who recruited Michael Hester to debate at West Georgia. Hester would extend Coach Gibson's legacy, first as a debater who was recognized as one of the top ten debaters at nationals three consecutive years and then later as the person to whom Coach Gibson would pass the baton.

In the quarter-century since Dr. Hester became the Director of Debate, West Georgia's debaters have won three national championships, finished runner-up twice, and reached the Elite Eight on five other occasions. As for Hester himself, he would twice be recognized with national coach of the year honors.

Throughout the tenure of both Coach Gibson and Dr. Hester, dozens of debaters would translate their debate lessons into the skills necessary to become successful attorneys, judges, educators, and public officials.

Randy took his debate experience and became a remarkably successful litigator. The very principles of analysis and communication that applied to convincing debate judges turned out to work in a courtroom both for winning jurors and for convincing judges. He won a remarkable number of very high-value cases both in jury trials and in convincing judges.

In the 44 years Randy and I have worked on campaigns together, his analytical skills have been amazing, and his strategic advice has been amazingly sound. When I had debates, I would turn to Randy for advice.

Like Abraham Lincoln and other successful lawyer-politicians, Randy understands that the juror and the voter are the same person. If you learn how to analyze and convincingly communicate with jurors, you have learned how to analyze and convincingly communicate with voters. He brought the Gibson principles to bear and found that they were remarkably powerful in indicating what would work and what would fail in each case.

My own experience with Coach Gibson's magic came when I was invited to the famed Oxford Union to debate the Vice President of Nicaragua Sergio Ramirez, on the Reagan policy of opposing communism in the Western hemisphere.

The Union has a long and storied history. It was founded in 1823. Its most famous vote was in 1933 when the Union passed its famous motion, "This House will in no circumstances fight for its King and Country" by 275 to 153. Britons divided angrily over that resolution, with Winston Churchill calling it "that abject, squalid, shameless avowal."

I knew going in that I would be up against a hostile crowd. I also knew that I did not understand the British style of debate. I promptly made a pilgrimage to Carrollton to get coaching from Chester Gibson. What he told me was beyond invaluable. It turned a potential disaster into a considerable victory.

"Look," Chester warned, "the British don't keep points for facts or for clever attacks. The British cherish humor. If you can make fun of your opponent in a way they can't answer, you have hit a home run. Be patient, be pleasant, and look for the opening."

I took that advice with me to Oxford (where Frank Luntz was a graduate student who participated in the debate and Boris Johnson, the future Prime Minister, was a student in the audience).

The students were very kind to me. It was an odd setting because Ramirez refused to debate and insisted that he give a speech and then leave. That left it up to the Oxford students on the pro-Nicaragua side to make the case.

Things had gone along okay but without a breakthrough until a really good-looking young guy got up and began making the case that the Reagan policy in Central America was not worthy of America. "I know America. I have lived in America. America is about more than baseball and hot dogs. America is about more than beaches and wet t-shirt contests."

I pounced instantly. I had been told that if the other side stood up, the presenter had an obligation to sit down and allow a question to be posed to them. I remembered vividly Coach Gibson's advice.

The young man was flustered, but under the rules, he had to sit down. When he did, I said slowly and with evident relish, "you are a good looking young man"—the audience began giggling—"indeed I would say that you are a very good looking young man"—now the audience was openly laughing and leaning forward to see where this was going.

"So, if you don't think America is about wet t-shirt contests"—and I paused—"how old were you when you were in America?" By this point his face was red, he was totally flustered, and then the audience began yelling "answer, answer."

He tried to bring the debate back to a serious point, but his situation was hopeless. I had followed the Gibson rule, and it had worked perfectly.

According to the *Los Angeles Times*, the Oxford Union President "said Gingrich spoke brilliantly and deserved the standing ovation he received from the crowd of more than 1,000 people.

"Ramirez got his (ovation) because of what he represented," Rudd said. "Gingrich earned his by sheer brilliance."

That brilliance had a name—it was Chester Gibson.

Note that this victory came as a result of paying attention to rules that were particular to that moment and that place.

There are two keys to really using this superb collection of rules and principles for successful debating.

The first key is to remember that different principles and different rules apply in different places, and you have to be acutely aware of the context in which you are working. The same principle may be great in one setting and ineffective or a disaster in another setting. Which leads to the second key.

You have to practice and practice and practice. It is just like being a great golfer or a good writer or an effective salesperson. The more you practice, the better you will get. The more you practice, the deeper you will understand and absorb the principles that work.

This is a great book to start debating with and if you come back to it again and again, you will become a dramatically more effective debater.

Randy and I can vouch for it from a lifetime of experience.

— Newt Gingrich

CHAPTER 1

WHY POLITICAL DEBATES MATTER

Age had become an issue in the 1984 election for President of the United States. President Ronald Reagan, seeking re-election, was in 1984 the oldest candidate for President in United States history. He had stumbled in his first debate with Walter Mondale, the Democratic nominee and former Vice President of the United States.

Age was certain to be an issue for the seventy-three-year-old incumbent President in the second debate; polls and punditry suggested vulnerability. Regardless of whether former Vice President Mondale or a questioner raised the issue, age was certain to be a topic on October 21, 1984, at the second presidential debate in the 1984 presidential election.

It did not take long once the ninety-minute debate got underway in Kansas City, Missouri. Technically, the topic for the debate was defense and foreign policy issues.

Yet, age and competence fit easily within the boundaries of any debate topic. Even if outside the boundaries of an agreed topic, nothing precluded anyone from raising the age issue in the context of dealing with foreign powers and protecting the national security of the United States.

Once it was his turn in the rotation of reporters asking questions, Henry "Hank" Trewhitt of the *Baltimore Sun* jumped right to it and asked President Reagan if he had any doubt that he was up to the job to serve again. Interestingly, Trewhitt raised President Reagan's older age in the context of the United States' youngest President, John F. Kennedy, and the Cuban Missile Crisis.

In responding, President Reagan did not hesitate. It was clear he knew the question in some form was coming, and he was well prepared with his response. And, undoubtedly, he knew that his response could well determine the direction of the election—would it be a contest or a blowout?

President Reagan responded succinctly and directly, making clear that he could serve just as President Kennedy had. But then President Reagan went further. He recognized the moment as an opportunity to put the issue to rest permanently, and he was not going to miss his chance.

So President Reagan, with the timing one would expect of a veteran actor, said, "and I want you to know that also I will not make age an issue of this campaign. I am not going to exploit, for political purposes, my opponent's youth and inexperience." The audience exploded with laughter. Even his opponent, former Vice President Mondale, and the reporter asking the question both chuckled.

The moment was so definite that Trewhitt, the questioner, had to wait for the laughter to die down before concluding, "Mr. President, I'd like to head for the fence and try to catch that one before it goes over." But it was too late. It was a home run.

It was the combination of content and style delivered with uncanny timing, redefining a critical issue on terms that not only put the issue to rest but more importantly, eliminated it from the contest. A single debate moment had altered the trajectory of the 1984 presidential election.

Rather than a close contest between an aging, struggling incumbent President bumbling his way through the campaign (including the debates), the election was not even close, as a confident President shed one of his largest vulnerabilities head-on with well-timed humor.

Pundits and pollsters uniformly agree that it was, and will forever be, a pivotal moment. Even Vice President Mondale would later confirm that he knew at that moment of the debate the impact it had and would have on the election to come.

The exchange reflects, indeed confirms, the power of modern political debate. That was over three decades ago. But even today, voters who watched that debate remember that moment.

Debates between candidates have become a tradition of the campaign season over the last half-century, with every presidential contest since the 1976 race between Carter and Ford including at least one televised debate (usually several). With tens of millions of television viewers, presidential debates top the list of campaign events that attract the greatest attention of the American public.

Although debates between candidates running for other elective offices—U.S. Congress and those at the state or local levels—do not attract the same volume of viewers, they have also become more commonly performed by, and generally expected of, candidates.

As a result of their historical significance and contemporary frequency, political debates have been the focus of myriad scholarly and journalistic perspectives. Analysis of the debates in the 1858 Illinois Senate race between Abraham Lincoln and Stephen Douglas alone generates thousands of search hits in Google Scholar.

Since the first televised debate between John F. Kennedy and Richard Nixon in 1960, presidential debates—those occurring between candidates running for president of the U.S.—in both their party's primary and the general election—and those for vice president, have received the most attention from researchers.

Scholars in the fields of Rhetoric, Political Science, and other academic disciplines have analyzed these contests from various angles: their influence on electoral outcomes, audience receptivity to particular messaging, how candidates treat each other and whether those behaviors are influenced by the candidates' identities, the significance and changing roles of news media in moderating the contests and reporting on them after the fact, even analyzing how the evolution in mass communication technology has affected debates.

In contrast, popular media's analysis of presidential debates has been more routinized, with nearly every news outlet that covers the debates producing its own "top ten list of greatest/worst moments" articles. The soundbite potential—both for boosting *and* for deflating candidates—of debates as political spectacle make them irresistible to media coverage. Reporting on the minutiae of campaign platforms and policy proposals is so much more difficult than spotlighting "zingers"or engaging in beauty pageant-level evaluations of which candidate sweat too much, blinked too little, or committed the crime of forgetting the name of a foreign leader.

All these analyses of presidential debates have their value in American society. In a 21st century democratic republic, seeking information that can help citizens be smarter voters is a worthy goal for academic research and media focus. For these reasons, we include many of these sources in the bibliography at the end of this book and encourage those who want to learn more about these subjects to check them out.

For those in the business of coaching candidates to win debates and the subsequent elections, the wide variety of perspectives on presidential debates is a sign that our work is not in vain. However, this book is not a rehash of those perspectives.

This book exists to accomplish a very different objective. It is written for those who want to learn how to *win* political debates—for the candidates and campaign teams trying to optimize their electoral chances; for the consultants searching for best practices that they can peddle to candidates; for the political junkies who are always excited to learn more about the inner workings of political campaigns; and, yes, even for the "ordinary" citizens who would like to learn more about why candidates do what they do on stage. After reading this book, you will think of political debates differently than you ever have before.

In the following chapters, a detailed account of the best practices for successful navigation of political debates will be presented, breaking down what candidates should (and should *not*) do in debates, as well as what campaign teams should consider when negotiating logistical details with debate hosts, media outlets, and the opposition. Whenever possible, examples from actual debates will be used to illustrate points and validate the accuracy of the advice being given.

Because of the national significance of presidential debates (and their place in the general public collective memory), nearly all of the examples provided are from the three types of presidential debates: primary debates between presidential candidates of the same party; general election debates between candidates who have successfully won their party's nomination; and vice presidential debates, which occur between individuals chosen to be second-in-command by the candidate at the top of the ticket.

CHAPTER 2

THE BEGINNING

Although tempting, the origins, evolution, and role of political debate cannot be skipped by anyone serious about winning through political debate. Many observers, especially cable news pundits, believe they fully understand political debate and, thus, are fully capable of commenting on, judging, and even debating extremely well themselves.

Political debate, as a generic proposition, does seem pretty straightforward; dictionary.com defines "debate" as "a formal discussion on a particular matter in a public meeting or legislative assembly, in which opposing arguments are put forward and which usually ends in a vote."

In the context of political debates, this translates to candidates seeking elected office engaging in a contest of ideas, moderated by a neutral observer, in which they extol the worthiness of their candidacy by advocating for their policy agenda and arguing against the policy agenda of their opponent. However, those with experience in academic debate and/or political campaigns will quickly concede that political debates are very different in both format and objectives.

A better starting point for understanding modern political debate might be understanding what political debate is not —how it is not "argument" and how it's not "debate" in the academic sense. For example, the communication of a disagreement without more does not constitute a "debate."

While it may seem inconsequential (whether something is a "debate"), it is actually a very important distinction for debate preparation and execution. In practice, debates can consist of arguments, but arguments are not themselves debates.

Monty Python's "Argument Clinic" illustrates the point. Those unfamiliar with the sketch from *Monty Python's Flying Circus*, written by John Cleese and Graham Chapman, should take a look to see the point that simple contradiction of whatever someone else is saying is not even an argument, much less a debate.

In the sketch, a customer enters a room, having paid for an "argument." Basically, once he gets to the right room, the person simply contradicts whatever he says. Eventually, the wordplay devolves down to sentences consisting of simple subject/verb pairs with no meaning except to reject whatever has been said.

(Notably, the text of the skit has been cited as an example of how not to argue as opposed to how to advance thought through a verbal discussion of the critical analysis of an issue. It certainly illustrates how not to "debate." Often, professional debate coaches play the sketch at the outset to show debaters what not to do.)

What focus groups and voters confirm is that, even on cable news or radio talk shows, the simple contradiction of the other debater's argument—no matter how loud or insulting the retorts get—hurts more than it helps. If the goal is to persuade or even just entertain debate viewers, then much more is required. And that is where understanding the origins and evolution of debate matters.

At the foundation of this book is an assumption born of experience: preparation matters. Yes, it is true that many of the skills we think of as being key traits of a great debater, including eloquence in the form of smooth delivery and mastery of memorable phrasing, or the ability to think quickly and adapt "on the fly," are frequently "natural gifts" of talented speakers who seemingly were born with a silver tongue.

Yet, the list of such intuitively-talented individuals who are also running for elected office is infinitesimal compared to the long list of actual candidates each cycle. As many campaign managers and political consultants learn when they begin working with their candidate, Ronald Reagan is not walking through that door, and Bill Clinton is not walking through that door.

Every presidential election after 1972 has included debates between candidates, regardless of whether that cycle's office seekers were talented speakers or not.

Actual debates against skilled and trained debaters prove natural talent practiced over time is not enough.

The good news is smart preparation does improve performance. Senator Mitt Romney is an apt example. After repeatedly suffering poor performances in the 2012 Republican presidential primary debates, he recognized he needed professional help.

To the shock of many, candidate Mitt Romney hired a debate coach for assistance during the 2012 GOP presidential debates. Now, like many candidates worried about being perceived as curated by "handlers," Senator Romney did not want anyone to know, and when the coach disclosed his role, Romney promptly dismissed him. But he did not do so until he had his two best debate performances in Florida and turned his campaign for the 2012 Republican presidential nomination around.

His first debate against President Barack Obama during the 2012 general election campaign is a perfect example of what smart preparation can achieve, as Romney was widely recognized for winning while Obama was panned for being unprepared and seemingly unmotivated (the incumbent's recovery in subsequent debates was attributed to taking the following debates more seriously and further confirms the importance of proper preparation).

It is crucial to distinguish what we are calling "political debates" from their academic counterparts and the activity of candidates on the stage from the formal argumentation taught in classes on rhetoric. More akin to "dueling press conferences," political debates are a unique public spectacle within the overall process we understand as political campaigns. They are the only moments in what has become a process extending beyond twelve months during which opposing candidates share the same stage—that fact alone signals their symbolic potential.

More significantly, for the purposes of this book, the academic disciplines of debate and argumentation do not represent, in any meaningful way, the skills necessary to win a political debate. Watching, studying, and copying the exchanges of intercollegiate debaters typically does more harm than good.

Indeed, these scenarios are only useful for identifying examples of what not to do rather than what *to* do to win a political debate. Even the classic "political debate shows" (e.g., *Evans and Novak*, the *McLaughlin Group*, and CNN's *Crossfire*) offer little in terms of useful tips for candidates preparing for political debates.

If viewers think about their own reactions after watching these shows, they would likely themselves recognize that these (often loud and sometimes incomprehensible) exchanges accomplished little. It is why no one really thinks that much gets done at the end of a day on the typical cable news program full of shouting, arguments, and confrontations. Discourse is rarely advanced, and there are rarely winners or losers.

However, these examples—academic debate competitions and political debate TV shows—do share one thing in common with political debates. All of them are grounded in a principle of American democracy with a long tradition: that public discussion and contestation of ideas is vital to a functioning society. The founding of the nation is replete with examples of this belief in the power of persuasion, with the Constitutional Convention of 1787 being among the most significant.

While the origins of the United States of America as a nation are most closely associated with the Revolutionary War in which the thirteen colonies successfully fought for their freedom from the British Crown, the government we consider the United States was actually formed not out of war but out of debate. The founders who gathered to discuss the inadequacies of the Articles of Confederation and exited having drawn up an entirely new structure of federal government changed their world not with swords but with words.

More recently, in a twentieth century that started with two world wars and ended with an impressive lack of global conflagration, this emphasis on using peaceful discussion and debate as a superior alternative has been at the heart of international organizations, such as the United Nations and the World Trade Organization. Their flaws notwithstanding, the reduction in world wars is commendable.

This evolution of progress-producing civil discourse has steadily and increasingly gravitated toward systematized

exchanges of ideas in forums with rules backed by political
governance for conflict resolution (as opposed to just weapons and armies). Notably, the common denominator for sub-
stituting words for weapons has been "debate"—in fact, "political debate."

Hence, political debate has become an essential pillar for
peaceful advancement of civilized societies, notwithstanding
a more and more complex world. That it has and why it has is
important to mastering the very art of political debate.

After all, on its best day, political debate is considered by
many people as grossly inefficient and even outright annoying.
Yet virtually everyone agrees that political debate is better
than any other alternative for meaningful dispute resolution
after due consideration to all possibilities.

Debate permits the airing of grievances, exploration of
ideas, advancement of critical thinking, development of
solutions, and the creation of political systems to govern.
So, every candidate dreading the very idea of appearing on a
stage for a political debate should remember the alternative
—a duel!

As U.S. Secretary of Treasury Alexander Hamilton and
Vice President Aaron Burr proved, duels do not work so well
for meaningful and final dispute resolution. Neither the victor
(Burr) nor the victim (Hamilton) ever recovered from their
duel (although the latter has made quite the comeback as the
muse for Broadway musicals!). Yet, even as recent as 2004,
Senator Zell Miller challenged MSNBC host Tim Russert to
a duel, and so our more violent instincts have not yet been
completely vanquished.

Debate has emerged as the superior alternative to physical conflict—and for good reason. It can produce lasting,
meaningful resolution of genuine disagreements without

bloodshed. Political debate can do the same in systems that contemplate such decisions in the context of democracies in which the will of those governed are involved.

Of course, political debate is not always an option. One need not list all the historical examples where "talking it out" simply was not feasible in order to acknowledge there is a time and place for political debate. The good news for citizens of the United States is that our political process affords us the privilege to exist in a society where political debate is available as an option for resolving disputes and influencing decisions.

As such, political debates between candidates have become a traditional component of campaign seasons. Candidates opposing each other for an elected office agree to participate in good faith, following predetermined guidelines negotiated by all sides.

While President Franklin Roosevelt once declined an invitation to debate Thomas Dewey and there were no presidential debates in the 1964, 1968, and 1972 election years, the last 44 years have cemented an expectation that presidential candidates will participate in *multiple* debates during their runs for office. The backlash of negative publicity from refusing to debate one's opponent is a risk that no presidential candidate would take in today's political climate.

Fortunately, no candidate in a political debate operates completely at the mercy of their opponent or debate host. Instead, each participant controls, in part, their own destiny through their own contributions to the process—thereby influencing, if not directing, the ultimate outcome.

It is not uncommon for negotiations over the logistical details of a debate event to be as contested as any points made during the debate itself. In addition to questions regarding the setting (location? audience size and selection? which candidates are invited to participate?), these negotiations are when the rules of the debate are agreed upon.

As the term suggests, "political debate" involves debate in the political world. Most often, it occurs in connection with elections—whether involving candidates or involving issues. Of course, political debate is nothing new.

Although political debates pre-dated even the existence of the United States, they became prominent in the Continental Congresses, leading up to the adoption of the Declaration of Independence. Similarly, political debates were at the essence of the writing and adoption of the United States Constitution.

Once convened, both the United States House of Representatives and the United States Senate institutionalized political debate as part of their deliberative process. Not all political debates reflect the civility typically attributed to the idea of civil discourse. Yet, it perseveres.

Political debates would take center stage in American elections with the Lincoln-Douglas debates. In 1858, Abraham Lincoln would challenge incumbent Illinois Senator Stephen Douglas in a series of seven debates.

The rules were much different at that time for political debate. In the Lincoln-Douglas debates, each candidate opened for one hour and the other then got a ninety-minute rebuttal (a format almost unfathomable in contemporary times!). The debates were so popular that they became huge events, drawing people from all around the country.

Senator Douglas would win re-election, but then lose to Lincoln in the 1860 presidential election. While the outcomes of the election contests were significant, the most significant historical consequence of Abraham Lincoln's debate challenge to Senator Stephen Douglas was that political debates became a part of the American political scene.

The first presidential debate appears to be between Thomas Dewey and Harold Stassen in a presidential primary debate (Oregon) in 1948. It was broadcast on radio. In the following twelve years, there would be three other presidential primary debates.

All of that changed in 1960 with the first televised presidential debate between then-Senator John F. Kennedy and then-Vice President Richard M. Nixon. The details of the debates, including all of the negotiations associated with them, are set forth in detail in *The Great Debates, Kennedy vs. Nixon 1960* (Indiana University Press 1962). For readers interested in just how much is involved in staging debates at the highest level, it is an impressive work.

Then there was a sixteen-year hiatus of presidential debates until President Gerald R. Ford debated President Jimmy Carter. Because of a gaffe by President Ford, the debate took on special significance, as every candidate (especially challengers to incumbent presidents such as President Ford) has insisted on presidential debates.

Since then, debates have been so permanently engrained that the Commission on Presidential Debates was formed for the sole purpose of setting the dates, times, places, and rules of presidential debates. But the impact now extends well beyond presidential debates.

Virtually every competitive election contest now often involves some form of a political debate (or at least demands for them) at every level of government. Presidential, gubernatorial, senatorial, and congressional debates are now routine.

In the world of cable news and social media, with tens

of millions of viewers and followers, there is an insatiable appetite for more. The bottom line is that political debates are simply a fact of political life.

Against that backdrop, candidates and campaigns now must prepare for and participate in political debate. Effective preparation and participation depend on proven effective tools that extend well beyond what happens on the stage during the debate itself.

To best understand and use these tools, remember: from the beginning of speech until today, the essential element that distinguishes meaningless argument from "debate" is the existence of rules.

And debate in the context of an election is "political debate" with its own implications and techniques for achieving that which is most important: winning on Election Day.

CHAPTER 3

RULES AND NORMS

Importance of Rules

Generally, as speech through verbal (both written and oral) communication has evolved, so has debate. Things that work have been used by each new generation of debaters to become more and more effective.

Some techniques that date as far back as Socrates (circa 400 BC) remain among the most effective ways to win debates today, while other tactics have been developed in response to changes in technology (with the proliferation of social media promising further evolution in political debate best practices). In all cases, however, the employment of effective debating tools and facilitating expressions of differing opinions actually prove quite effective in finding solutions and reaching consensus on important issues.

In the context of political debate, the tools can do even more. They can credential, persuade, motivate, and influence thought—most importantly, the thoughts and opinions of voters. And in nearly every case, they leverage the essential element of debate—rules.

At the risk of stating the obvious, rules govern debate. Participant requirements shape the arguments, presentations, and communicated ideas in an effort to advance an idea, proposal, or resolution. This is a critically important point for debaters' preparation and performance. In a very real sense, the rules that define the debate determine what are and are not good debate practices.

Regardless of whether arguments occur on university campuses or floor debates in the United States Senate, the single distinguishing characteristic for meaningful "debate" are the rules defining what is and is not, allowed or required. To fully understand debate, the most important concept to understand is that, at its core, a debate is an argument with rules.

The evolution of debates and the rules that make them has been steady and well-documented. Just a quick review of the rules for the House of Commons or the United States Senate vividly illustrates the constant expansion of the number, kind, and scope of debate rules for the articulation, discussion, evolution, and resolution of contested issues. Today, there are professionals who do nothing but specialize in rules, like those in *Robert's Rules of Order Newly Revised* (11th Edition), governing debate.

It is not some specific single rule that converts an argument into a debate; rather, it is the existence of a set of rules. Consider board games—what makes Monopoly different from Parcheesi? The rules establishing how the game is to be played.

In political debates, the rules can limit time, guarantee both sides the right to speak, or restrict the topics. Or the rules can do none of these things. But to be a debate, there must be rules. An argument occurs whenever at least two sides articulate disagreement on a proposition. A *debate* occurs when at least two sides agree to argue within boundaries accepted by all sides.

Creating, making, defining, and construing these rules is

the foundation upon which every other strategy depends. It is why the two most important committees in the United States House of Representatives and Senate are the House Rules Committee and the Senate Rules Committee.

In the academic setting, the rules of debate are quite different. In the United States, at the collegiate level, there are even different rules for different kinds of competitive intercollegiate debate, which then govern all national competitions.

Though they frequently follow a somewhat standardized format, the rules for political debates are negotiated in advance for each election contest and can result in very different events (the addition of "townhall" debates in the last thirty years is an example of such modifications).

Norms of Behavior

The negotiated rules are not the only guidelines governing the candidates on stage. Just when candidates think they have a good handle on the written rules or at least access to them, there are the unwritten (even unspoken) rules of conduct that are ever-changing as societal norms evolve. No better example exists than "behaving on stage." Who exactly knows what that means?

Two debates involving former First Lady Hillary Clinton illustrate the blurred lines of behavioral norms. In the 2000 New York Senate race to succeed Senator Daniel Patrick Moynihan, former Congressman and Senate candidate Rick Lazio faced off against former First Lady and Senate candidate Hillary Clinton.

In an intentional move in a September 13, 2000, debate, Lazio left his podium and walked over to then-candidate

Clinton to ask her to sign a document affirming a pledge to abstain from benefiting from "soft money." Clinton refused. Oops—that violates the "do not invade the other candidate's space" rule.

Lazio much later said he regretted his approach. It dominated coverage of the debate with little discussion of anything else that was said. He lost, and the former First Lady of the United States became the United States Senator from New York.

Lazio, upon reflection, had to ask himself when the reaction to his debate tactic started to air: where did that reaction come from? After all, there was no rule stating that the candidates had to stay at their podiums.

Indeed, sixteen years later in a presidential debate versus former Senator Clinton, then-Republican candidate for President Donald Trump would frequently move into place behind his opponent (and into the camera angle of Clinton as she responded to the moderator's question). While multiple news outlets questioned his behavior, which was described as "prowling" and "looming," candidate Trump's ascension to President Trump showed that his violation of debate norms did not carry with it the same negative consequences.

The issue of violating the personal space of one's opponent has not been limited to races between candidates of different genders. For example, the 2000 general election presidential debates between President George W. Bush and Vice President Albert Gore (both men) involved different settings and formats.

The second debate on October 17, 2000, at Washington University in St. Louis, Missouri, was a townhall-style debate with stools for the candidates on opposite ends of the stage.

The debate was moderated by Jim Lehrer of PBS. It was televised by MSNBC.

Each candidate remained seated on their stool in their respective corners during most of the debate while the other candidate spoke. There were times when each candidate would stand and even move about slightly. But then, there came a moment when all that changed.

While President George W. Bush was answering a question about the differences between the two candidates, Vice President Gore suddenly stood up from his stool, and walked decidedly toward President Bush. Unlike other occasions, he clearly approached President Bush and everyone—both in the audience and at home—noticed.

As Vice President Gore reached him on the stage, President Bush acknowledged him with direct eye contact and a decided nod, highlighting the Vice President's presence, and continued. The audience laughed; it was not a good moment for Vice President Gore. He tried to recover with his own question to President Bush, but it fell flat.

Given that the 2000 presidential election was one of the closest elections in history, decided by a few hundred votes and requiring a Supreme Court ruling to settle the matter, it is not an exaggeration to suggest that this mistake may have cost Vice President Albert Gore the heaviest price.

Considering their potential effects on the outcomes of elections, these unwritten rules can cause concern and anxiety. For candidates preparing for debates, there are many questions: where can one learn about these norms? How is a candidate supposed to know? What is the penalty for violating the rule? And why do some candidates get penalized while others do not?

As daunting as these abstract norms of behavior may be for candidates, there are ways to prepare for them. Ultimately, the goal for candidates and their campaigns is to eliminate (or at least reduce) as many of these violations of norms as possible. Later in this book, we will cover several best practices regarding how candidates should behave on stage.

Negotiation of Rules

Another way to reduce the risks of violating unwritten rules is to turn them into *written* rules to explicitly govern behavior during the debate. For example, the debate rules could include a requirement stating that, when not speaking, candidates should remain on their stool. Then no one cares, and those that do care have no standing to raise the issue since it is covered by a rule.

Notice the consistent theme—rules. The existence of rules can be a candidate's best friend. Similarly, the absence of rules can be a candidate's worst enemy. Of course, if there are too many rules, the spontaneity of debate can be lost, and the debate becomes as dull as dirt. On the other hand, a debate dulled by restrictive rules may be exactly what a heavily favored candidate wants when debating against an unknown challenger.

The bottom line is the rules matter, and they matter a lot. Given the singular importance of rules for successful political debate, it is hard to even imagine that many candidates actually leave the rules to someone else.

Sometimes, campaign officials simply accept the rules received from a debate sponsor or a media outlet. Others skip the discussion altogether. Without question, it is a terrible mistake for a candidate to make regarding political debates

—letting someone else, either the moderator/media or, worse yet, the opposing candidate set the rules by default.

Always participate in creating the rules, and in that process, insist on rules that help the candidate and oppose rules that jeopardize them. Leave as few issues open as possible. Knowing what can and cannot be done before a debate is so much better than learning on the stage.

To understand the importance of debate rules, consider how much rules matter for elected officials engaged in governance. Watch the fierce floor fights in both the United States House and Senate over the rules for debate. These debates are often fiercer than the debate on the bill or resolution itself. It is why the most powerful committees in the United States House of Representatives and Senate are the Committee on Rules in the House of Representatives and the Committee on Rules and Administration in the Senate.

At the other end of the spectrum, the best opportunity to protect (or expose) a weak candidate or empower (or neutralize) a strong candidate in a political debate is in the creation of the rules for the debate. Rules are not only effective tools for defense of a candidate; rules are effective tools for empowering a candidate to go on offense against an opponent in an election.

With a blank slate to start, the timing, duration, sitting or standing, length of answers, right to replies, opening, closing, questioning of other candidates, and every other aspect of the political debate are all subject to regulation by rules—or not. No good reason exists for a candidate to take the stage with so many open issues.

In the end, the boundaries of political debate rules are limited only by the imagination and creativity of those making them. The Rules for the 2016 Presidential Debates is an exhaustive list of topics and rules. Every candidate and their team can look through them and see what does apply and what does not. Although it may seem daunting, not even considering the possibilities (with such a resource readily available) is a bad idea.

As reflected by the Rules themselves, no one should be surprised at the depth of deliberations associated with presidential debates and the scope and extent of the rules to which presidential candidates agreed as reflected by the sheer length of the Presidential Debate Rules. By the time the professionals are done, everything from whether a candidate can use a notepad to whether they can stand on a footstool has been carefully vetted, considered, and addressed. When video/television is added, a whole new set of issues and rules come into play (think of how "TV timeouts" affect the flow of sports).

Of course, if both candidates are well-represented, neither candidate will get everything they wanted. Instead, like any good negotiation that produces an agreement, there will be a significant amount of give and take. Each side must determine what are the most important rules they want (or want to avoid) and concede ground on the details they deem less important. Obviously, the most important factors in making those decisions are the relative strengths and weaknesses of the candidate in a debate format.

For example, mentally quicker candidates typically want more interaction for sparring with and rebutting their opponent's claims directly. Policy-wonk candidates often want longer openings/closings and answers so they can penetrate past the sound bites and get into the merits. Candidates with strong interpersonal skills tend to enjoy the more intimate feel and audience interaction that comes with the townhall format.

Candidates who feed off the energy of large crowds will want an audience to which they can play, whereas candidates whose strength lies more in policy-making than crowd-pleasing may prefer a setting in which the candidates and moderator sit around a table, with no live audience at all. It is all about tailoring the specific debate rules to each individual candidate and their strengths.

With so many possibilities, where is the best place to start in negotiating the best rules for a particular candidate in a specific election contest in an upcoming election cycle? Well, it begins with answering the broader question of what is the objective for the campaign and, correspondingly, for the political debate? It sounds simple enough—win the debate! So long as doing so contributes to winning the election.

It is true that winning debates alone rarely have any significant impact on the outcome of an election. Most voters cannot even remember when they vote who won or lost a debate, and for those that do remember, it is virtually never a factor in their decision for whom to vote.

Indeed, if being the best debater dictated election outcomes, then the government would be populated primarily with great debaters. Yet, one quick glance of C-SPAN for ten minutes confirms to anyone who watches that the best debaters are not in government.

Although "winning the debate" will likely be *an* objective, it should never be *the* objective. A debate will include multiple aims to prove something—something about the candidate, the opponent, the issues, the election, reasons for voting, or something else. Simply proving that a candidate can actually stand up in front of a camera for an hour discussing important issues without looking foolish can be an objective.

With that in mind, never look past the single most important objective for every campaign: *winning the election.* So, maybe, indeed probably, the starting point is obvious: what will help win the election?

From that overarching objective, many other goals will then bubble up, creating a multi-pronged debate strategy. Accomplishing all of them may be too much to expect. But checking the box for as many as possible is a great start.

Every successful debate strategy has at its core a simple open-ended inquiry that cannot be repeated enough: *what can be accomplished in the political debate that will increase the candidate's ability to win the election?* Keep it at the top of every pad, chalkboard, and computer screen.

The overarching goal is and should always be to win the election. Everything else is secondary. Using political debate to accomplish that objective will often be one of the most effective tools in the campaign's arsenal.

CHAPTER 4

THE OBJECTIVE

When Speaker Newt Gingrich was a young Congressman, he represented a sprawling congressional district that stretched from South Atlanta all the way to the Alabama border. It included everything from the Atlanta airport to the most rural farmlands of western Georgia, with a college and military base included.

Undoubtedly, his greatest vulnerability was in the heaviest concentration of voters in a single county south of Atlanta—Clayton County. While this one county electorally dominated his district, the fact was his congressional district actually included fifteen counties, of which Clayton County was but one.

Many of the counties were so small that they were numerically smaller than some of the precincts in Clayton County. But, as any good Member of Congress should, he vehemently insisted that every county was important (implicitly suggesting that every county was equally important).

So, every election cycle, Congressman Gingrich would begin his campaign for re-election with a simple challenge for his opponent: to debate in each and every county. Rather unbelievably, but routinely, most challengers would then agree. The two campaigns would then set out to negotiate a schedule that included fifteen debates—one per county in the district.

With most election seasons back then beginning after Labor Day, that left a little more than two months of peak campaign season. But, for all practical purposes, fifteen of those precious days would be spent traveling and debating in some part of the district that would have little chance of making a difference.

Of course, a debate involved much more than just the candidates. There would inevitably be a campaign event, volunteers deployed, and money spent—a lot of it in places no challenger wanted to be weeks before the election. But it was not just challengers stuck in this predicament.

Many pundits interpreted Congressman Gingrich's challenge as an indication of his overconfident reliance on his exceptional debate skills. Of course, if the worst thing the pundits could say about him was that Congressman Gingrich was a great debater or an overconfident politician, he was coming out ahead.

Make no mistake: he was a skilled and talented debater, a reputation he earned on the campaign trail—first for Congress, then for Minority Whip, and ultimately as Speaker of the House. He would carry that reputation into debates at Cambridge and with Senator John Kerry over climate change.

Speaker Gingrich never took a single debate for granted, even those after his time in Congress. He started early in his career with debate preparation and training with the assistance of Dr. Chester Gibson, chair of the Mass Communications Department at what was then West Georgia College, where Gingrich had once been a faculty member in the History department.

Dr. Gibson was nationally renowned as a debate coach, having transformed the small college into a true national debate powerhouse that competed successfully against schools such as Harvard, Northwestern, and UCLA. Speaker Gingrich would use every free moment to study the materials, practice debating, and master the art of political debate.

However, Congressman Gingrich's defiant challenge to his opponents to debate in every county in the congressional district actually had nothing to do with his confidence on the debate stage. Instead, it had everything to do with the single most important strategy for every candidate: winning the next election. Each time an opponent accepted Congressman Gingrich's debate challenge, they agreed to go to every part of the congressional district except the one place they needed to spend the most time—Clayton County, where the most voters were.

With thousands of voters concentrated in one place, challengers would spend roughly a quarter of the peak campaign season going somewhere else. They would dutifully appear in a very small county with few voters (and even fewer voters showing up for the debate).

There might be an article in the small county's local newspaper but not much else. This was because few reporters had the time to travel to all parts of the district. They had their day jobs reporting on local events in the county in which they lived and worked. It did not make sense to expend the resources to cover other counties, especially distant small counties with which their home county had little in common.

Notably, all of this was well before social media and the internet connecting all the world, including small rural counties with larger suburban counties in Georgia. It was also before Speaker Gingrich would be so well known that he was a story all to himself.

In 1978, the Sixth Congressional District was a sleepy sprawling congressional district that came nowhere close to meriting national media coverage. It did not even merit regional media coverage. The impact of Congressman Gingrich's strategy was magnified immensely by nature of the congressional district itself.

When these far-flung debates occurred, no one in the county that mattered the most heard or saw much of anything from the challenger. Even reporters who may have been attracted by the idea of taking Congressman Gingrich down a peg lost interest when the debates were often one-sided affairs with Congressman Gingrich dominating the discussion and the issues.

Speaker Gingrich was first elected in 1978 and reelected a total of nine times, including five times in his original fifteen-county district (until redistricting occurred prior to the 1992 election). Speaker Gingrich retired in 2001. After his 1978 election win, Speaker Gingrich was never defeated at the ballot box.

Did his strategy of debating in every county in the district help him achieve the prime objective of winning the next election? Undoubtedly, it did. Indeed, his first re-election was very close, and many believe that if his opponent had spent more time in the county or counties where voters actually lived, Congressman Gingrich would have never survived his first bid for re-election.

Of course, it is an insightful example of just how political debate can help with the objective of winning the election without involving anything that actually happens in the political debates themselves. The fact was that Congressman Gingrich's use of political debate was less about what occurred in the debate and more about the impact the debates had on the campaign.

The lesson from Congressman Gingrich's strategy is

for candidates and campaigns to expand how they envision the role of political debates as part of their overall election strategy. Political debates can reach many more priorities than just jousting on the stage with an opponent. Political debate is much more than merely a necessary evil for getting to the election.

It can be and should be an important tool in advancing the overall election strategy for winning. This means candidates and campaigns must identify the key factors for success in winning the election and then determine which factors can be advanced through an effective political debate strategy. It is not as difficult as it may seem at first.

Most serious campaigns should have a campaign strategy delineating the key factors for winning on Election Day. Campaign strategy typically includes all sorts of election activities, including fundraising, publicity events, voter turnout, issue orientation, and of course social media in the 21st century. Political debates can and should be integrated into all these activities or, conversely, the political debate strategy should integrate all of these activities into each debate event.

In the modern political world, political debates can and should be real productions, with as many ancillary activities that the debate can support. This includes fundraising, volunteer events, voter registration as permitted, and any other activity that leverages the physical presence of a candidate, volunteers, and political entertainment.

Within this context, put the campaign's strategies for winning up on a wall or on a computer screen and then determine how many can be implemented in conjunction with a political debate. If the goal is to keep a challenger from concentrating time, energy, and resources on a critical county, insist on ground rules that require them to go everywhere else to debate.

While the litany of opportunities for leveraging debates are too numerous to even list (including fundraising, volunteer events, voter contacts, media, and issue orientation), it is important that none dominate over the real purpose for being there—a political debate. Candidates need to be fresh, rested, and focused when they take the stage, so any ancillary strategies should remain exactly that—ancillary—and be handled by other campaign staff.

The goal is to strike that fine balance between fully taking advantage of a campaign event with the candidate in attendance—the political debate—without jeopardizing or reducing the candidate's effectiveness at the debate. The right balance will obviously vary from candidate to candidate. Finding that balance involves objectively assessing the personal cost to the candidate's stamina, focus, and ability to deliver against the benefits gained from each additional activity added. If the costs outweigh the benefits, always err in favor of a strong debate performance.

CHAPTER 5

FORCING DEBATE

Traditional thinking has been that heavy favorites, typically incumbents and well-funded frontrunners, should avoid debates (sometimes at all costs), while challengers should try to get as many debates as possible. These assumptions are supported by reasonable generalizations about nearly every race.

Favorites typically already have name recognition, money, resources, and infrastructure. Challengers rarely have less of all of these and, in some cases, none of them. Political debates typically supply all of them, especially as the significance of the office sought goes up and the election contest gets closer.

Debates, almost by definition, put the challenger on equal footing with the favorite, at least for an hour or two. While on stage, all candidates are optically equal—standing together, speaking, and responding.

Absent a chyron by television, there is nothing on the television screen that reflects anything about the candidates, which means political debates offer the candidates a unique opportunity to speak for themselves. In all respects, assuming no unusual rules resetting the format to favor one candidate or the other, challengers get the same opportunity as the incumbent or favorite to talk directly to voters and the media.

Put in its most basic terms, political debates, especially televised political debates, are tantamount to a challenger getting to run a political advertisement (the opening), then a political advertisement every time the incumbent runs a political advertisement (responses), and a final political advertisement at the end (the closing)—all for free.

In political speak, debates are an example of what is called "earned media," since candidates "earn" it rather than pay for it. Obviously, no incumbent or frontrunner wants to give a challenger any free media. Conversely, all challengers want as much free media and exposure as possible. The more times challengers can get this opportunity to communicate directly with voters, the more opportunities they have to make up ground in the race.

Political debates impact something as basic as name recognition, which should improve with every debate. The repetition of each candidate's name throughout the debate for one to two hours, along with the news coverage using the candidates' names before the debate, during the debate, and after the debate is big. With social media, this coverage increases exponentially. These simple facts should not be overlooked.

Although everyone in the political world understood this, Republicans were the first at a national level to police it. Under the chairmanship of Reince Priebus, the Republican National Committee knew well the potential consequences of twenty unregulated debates throughout the primary nomination process.

Chair Priebus set up a special committee which adopted specific rules after consultation with the cable news and candidates, designed to create a more fair and meaningful debate process. Rather than allowing those most interested in ratings from "Jerry Springer"-type debates (cable news), the Subcommittee on Presidential Debates (a subcommittee of the powerful Rules Committee) considered, developed, and implemented rules for the primary debates.

The RNC Debate Rules covered many critical topics, including a schedule (giving many more candidates an opportunity for access to the benefits of the earned media associated with the debates); the moderators (to assure that the debates stayed relevant to issues important to voters in a Republican primary as opposed to red meat for on-air political fights); criteria for participation (to assure that everyone knew what was required long before the debate so that the candidates and their campaigns could adapt their strategies accordingly), and many more.

In 2016, when confronted with its own deluge of candidates, Democrats also turned to formalized rules for controlling the debate process. To be fair, both national political parties have had rules for debates for many years. The formalization and expansion of these rules has been a relatively new phenomenon as the roles of social media, cable news, and the number of candidates has increased.

Designing rules for intra-party (i.e., "primary") political debates, as opposed to a negotiated one among candidates from different parties in a general election, is a difficult balance. On the one hand, national political parties should never "rig" the process to favor one candidate or one set of candidates.

On the other hand, the rules do need to reflect political reality—which is that not every qualified candidate is a realistic or meaningful candidate, and each additional candidate makes the ability of those who are real much more difficult, if not impossible. Where the lines get drawn have serious consequences—indeed, the lines can dictate who makes it and who does not.

In the 2012 GOP primary debates, Republican presidential contenders fought hard to move from the "junior debate" (a second debate among second-tier candidates who did not reach the threshold for the debate among the top-tier candidates) to the "senior" debate. Fewer viewers tuned in for the junior debate and hence the ancillary benefits of the junior political debates were diminished.

To illustrate the impact of publicly televised debates (even on a single cable channel), former Senator Rick Santorum made his way from the junior debate to the senior debate and eventually the only debates among contenders for the 2012 GOP presidential nomination. In fact, he progressed all the way to the final three—eventual GOP nominee Senator Mitt Romney, former Senator Rick Santorum, and former Speaker Newt Gingrich.

To shift the nomination process closer toward a meritocracy as opposed to systemic favoritism for the next favorite up, the Republican National Committee seized control of the primary debates in 2016. Its Debate Subcommittee, in close consultation with the campaigns, media, and state political parties, established rules to govern the debates—including, importantly, scheduling. This contrasted sharply with previous election seasons, when the media dictated the rules, participants, and even schedule to fit their objectives (which may have contradicted those of the political parties).

Under the RNC Debate Subcommittee rules, the debates were spread out on the calendar based on the primary and caucus schedule. This approach gave every candidate—early favorites and those who were lesser-known, self-funders and populists, and all others meeting the debate criteria— infusions of celebrity and money based on their performance as opposed to their institutional standing in the party.

These rules confirmed the reality of the modern "political debate" phenomenon in the social media/cable news coverage world, and it applies regardless of political party or ideology. It is why missing the cut for the 2020 Democratic presidential debates was fatal to so many candidates. It is also why those dictating the criteria for making the stage have so much power.

Participating in nationally televised debates by its very nature drives up name recognition, volunteers, and fund-raising. The same is true at the state, congressional, and local levels.

Speaker Gingrich first demonstrated the cumulative impact of television with his one-minute speeches using just C-SPAN coverage. Add to it social media, and the impact is magnified. (Speaker Gingrich used GOPAC cassette tapes and the mail. Today, all of that content can be instantly communicated to thousands of voters.)

Many may believe that this modern political debate phenomenon is limited to national elections or high-profile contests. It is not. Yes, national debates, like pro football games, receive a lot of attention and commentary. But local elections, like local high school football teams, do too.

The truth is that the order of magnitude of the impact of a political debate to an election contest largely mirrors the magnitude of the election contest itself. Presidential debates in presidential elections matter a lot. To those who care, local school board debates in a local school board election also matter a lot.

Like C-SPAN two decades ago, local cable access channels now cover everything from county commission contests to mayors' races—even when most are not watching. On the other hand, as C-SPAN proved, media—live or reported—is media. With Twitter already in existence for more than a decade, Instagram "turning ten" by the time elections occur in November 2020, and everyone's grandmother having a Facebook account, the potential for political debates to help candidates gain the attention of voters is at an all-time high.

And, notably, as voters move closer and closer toward deciding for whom to vote, they tend to drift toward paying closer and closer attention to what is happening in the election contest. In some ways, it is like buying a car. No one really watches the automobile advertisements when they pop up. But, for those looking to buy a car, the advertisements suddenly become more interesting to watch.

But media alone should never be the only consideration when considering questions surrounding participation in a political debate. At some level, political debates still matter as a part of the process of winning the argument and winning over the hearts and minds of voters, including community thought leaders.

While not as significant as televised or print media, the fact is that "those in the know" can significantly impact the outcome of a local election contest. Ask any judge about the opinion of the local bar association and it will become clear that what is said and then repeated about candidates, especially after head-to-head competitions between candidates, is important.

Former British Prime Minister Margaret Thatcher once said: "First you win the argument, then you win the vote." Political debate is one effective way to do that. Earned and social media then only exponentially expand the political impact of winning the point, winning the argument, winning the debate, and winning the election.

The question then remains: with these dynamics at play, why would any favorite such as an incumbent or frontrunner ever give such a valuable potential asset to an opponent? Given the risks of a costly gaffe, why would any favorite stray into the potentially choppy waters from a political storm created by a serious mistake or error in a political debate?

Moreover, any political consultant or campaign manager recommending anything other than a resounding "No" would be unquestionably guilty of "political consulting malpractice" without more. As a result, the safe bet, and the one that has historically played out in election cycle after election cycle, has been "no debates" for incumbents and frontrunners. Of course, when the incumbent perceives their opponent is the frontrunner, this logic gets upended and they suddenly become very interested in having as many debates as possible!

It is also the case that some election contests do not have an incumbent. Due to term limits, retirements, and other factors, it does occasionally happen that there is no incumbent. Since President Barack Obama was term-limited, there was no incumbent in 2016 in either the Democratic or Republican national nomination process. When that happens, candidates and campaigns or, in some cases political parties, should seize the moment on political debates.

Challengers, with a lot of help from the media (who do like to sell the newspapers and draw the viewers to watch debates), have more tools available today to force debates than ever before. Social media, effectively applied, exponentially increases the pressure to force at least one, if not more, political debates.

Things that never worked in the past are now viable to force incumbents and favorites to agree to and even show up for political debates. Some of the ones most used have included empty chairs, carve-outs, empty podiums, chicken suits (that followed the other candidate around), and an assortment of public ridicule in different forums for being "afraid to debate."

Admittedly, they sound silly. But, when applied patiently, persistently, and effectively, they actually work. Integrate other grassroots strategies, and the chances increase that the ultimate pressure to appear for political debate becomes more than any candidate, even an incumbent or frontrunner, can ignore.

To be fair, fear of the challenger in a political debate generally has nothing to do with the decision of an incumbent's or favorite's refusal to debate. Most incumbents have little fear of a challenger on personal subjective terms. If anything, most incumbents feel contempt, not fear, of a challenger.

Incumbents may find it difficult to picture the challenger with any kind of equal footing on the debate stage. Yet, they know the political realities are that incumbents and frontrunners have far more to lose than gain in a political debate with an unknown, untested challenger.

Every underdog has the chance of an upset. Incumbents and frontrunners know this. So why would they ever give a challenger a platform they otherwise could never afford to buy, only to risk a costly mistake that could cost them their re-election?

There are exceptions. And, as President Donald Trump proved in the 2016 GOP presidential debates, it is possible to entirely skip a debate even in a crowded field and still win.

For those who may have forgotten, President Trump skipped a seemingly critical GOP presidential debate hosted by Fox News. He was the frontrunner at the time. He did not just skip any debate; he skipped the last debate before the all-important Iowa caucuses.

Citing unfair treatment by Fox News Channel host Megyn Kelly, the leading candidate skipped the debate and instead held a fundraiser for military causes. At the time, it was considered a high-stakes political poker move. In the end, it ended as a footnote in political history.

Notably, President Trump only skipped one. In addition, he knew that other debates were coming, as the RNC Debate Committee had negotiated and scheduled more debates and there was no penalty for skipping a sanctioned debate. There was only a penalty for participating in an unsanctioned debate.

Behind the scenes, he could not have been aware that there were the "never-Trumpers" who wanted to use his refusal to participate as a basis to ban him from any further debate. As history now reflects, those efforts failed. President Trump's success in skipping a debate is definitely the exception and not the rule. The onus remains on the challenger(s) to force the issue.

Most now agree in retrospect that both Fox News and the other GOP challengers would have been well served to have left his spot vacant and made the most of his absence. Instead, Senator Ted Cruz assumed the position of frontrunner, and the debate became a non-event. For good reason, it was not a risk that President Trump would take again.

Challengers intent on forcing debates have been known to appear at a place at the same time as the incumbent and attempt to force an impromptu debate. This never works. For one thing, there are no rules—an essential element for the debate. Without rules, there is no structure, no format, and largely without exception, no debate.

The best option for forcing a favorite or incumbent to debate is to put their motive for not debating at issue. It cannot be just that the incumbent or favorite is afraid to debate. The fact that the candidate is an incumbent or frontrunner is plenty proof that they have the standing to hold the office, and fear of the challenger is just not credible with either the media or most voters in that context.

Scandal, inappropriate conduct, unexplained absences, not voting, and investigations can be effective tools. But there must be some factual basis for putting these issues at play. Simply throwing them out there with no basis only serves to destroy any credibility that a challenger might have.

On the other hand, if bases do exist, then a challenger should put the incumbent or frontrunner's motives for avoiding debates at play and increase the pressure substantially to appear for a debate. Historically, the most effective technique is to put forth the question or questions (no more than three) that the challenger believes demand an answer and then stick to the question(s) repetitively until the incumbent either responds or agrees to a debate.

Patience is key. Every incumbent and frontrunner will ignore questions of this nature and every other kind until they cannot ignore them anymore. The pressure must steadily build based on a chorus of others insisting on answers to the questions as well. "Why have you missed so many committee meetings and so many votes, and now you will miss every opportunity to debate—why? Voters need an answer."

It also helps to build the pressure if the incumbent or frontrunner follows a similar pattern regarding other questions. Remember, most incumbents and frontrunners are playing what is called in football a "prevent defense." The only problem, as most football fans know well, is that prevent defenses can prevent the team that is ahead from *winning*!

In the political context, the "prevent defense" means that the incumbent really does not want to answer any questions from anyone. So, they tend to skip answering questionnaires from interest groups. Cumulatively, however, these dodges only add fuel to the fire.

For example, an unanswered questionnaire can translate into one more way to tell voters what they need to know, one more group of voters disenfranchised, and one more group that demands answers. If it grows into unanswered questionnaires, then the pressure mounts.

Once a challenger recognizes that an incumbent has decided to refuse to answer questionnaires, then push for more organizations and media outlets to send questionnaires (which will go unanswered by the incumbent). In the end, it will be the cumulative effect that forces an incumbent to the debate stage. Isolated pressure points rarely work.

And, because most of the media always want a debate, challengers can attempt to work with them to increase the pressure for a debate. Find a sponsor, lock down reporters, and agree on a date so that the only holdout is the incumbent or frontrunner.

Forcing a debate, and then forcing other debates will not come from just a demand from the challenger. There must be more. The pressure must build.

Typically, reluctant incumbents only agree to debate after a debate becomes inevitable. Because this build-up takes time, it is critically important that the effort begin early and remain constant. The "why will you not agree to debate" question must be a part of every strategy, communication, and tactic.

The earlier started, the better. It gives the challenger more time to apply more pressure. The end must appear inevitable, which means it must appear. Inevitability often takes the form of civic organization-sponsored debates on a certain date involving news reporters (and if possible, televised coverage).

While easily said, this inevitable political debate in the future actually has a lot of moving parts. To start, challengers must find a civic organization (not in the pocket of the incumbent or frontrunner) willing to invite an incumbent who is not going to be happy about getting an invitation to a debate the incumbent does not want.

One good starting point will be organizations that have sponsored debates in the past or organizations that have, as part of their core mission, a focus on elections and voter education (e.g., The League of Women Voters).

It is more difficult for an incumbent to reject an organization if it has sponsored debates in which the incumbent has participated before. Similarly, it is difficult for incumbents to reject debates from reputable civic organizations. The more reputable the organization, the more difficult it will be for the incumbent to say "No."

At a minimum, sponsorship by a reputable organization increases the costs to the incumbent for rejecting the debate. First, no politician wants to slight the good name of a reputable civic group. Moreover, there is the risk of alienating the organization's members by refusing the offer. All these factors add up to more pressure.

In addition, challengers must involve the media. Most times, this involves little more than offering specific reporters some meaningful role in the debate. It can be as moderator or as one of the panelists. Reporters like being important as much as anyone does. The key is to involve them to such an extent that they want the debate as much as the challenger does.

The first challenge to a debate should come from the sponsor, include the sponsor's name (with a bio) and the participating media's names—but nothing more. Specifying locations, dates, and times only give incumbents easy outs for saying no. Instead, invite the incumbent to give dates. It is difficult indeed for an incumbent to say "No" to a date that the incumbent supplied. Of course, it does happen.

If the incumbent objects to a sponsor or some member of the media, address it through the sponsor or, if necessary, a different sponsor. The goal is to get agreement by the incumbent on just two things: a debate and a date. Once those two things are in place, the challenger can focus on the details such as venue, location, and time.

Once the logistical details have been set, confirm the debate—repeatedly. The more times the existence of the agreed political debate, including the date, time, and location, are repeated the more difficult it becomes for the incumbent to back out.

Sometimes, incumbents and frontrunners choose to just ignore all efforts—including those by the sponsor and the media. Collectively and separately, the sponsor, media, and the challenger should make the incumbent pay for it. The refusal to debate should become a focal point—moving from the generic to the specific with the specific being "why will [the incumbent] not answer questions at a debate sponsored by a good organization by respected members of the media?"

Eventually, to truly put motive at play, effective challengers move the focus from the debate to something different: what is the incumbent hiding? Or, to personalize it, the question can shift to: what is the incumbent hiding from? The moment the election contest shifts from the issues to the incumbent personally, the greater the pressure is for an incumbent to show up.

To increase the pressure further, challengers sometimes up the ante by placing friendly wagers that the incumbent will never show up. When asked how the challenger can be so confident, the best response is to leave it to voters' imaginations with some innuendo about just how bad it must be.

Make the incumbent prove a negative, i.e., prove that nothing bad exists. Of course, the only way to actually prove the negative is to show up and debate. Anything else leaves all the possibilities on the table and maximizes the costs for the incumbent of refusing to show up and debate.

The beauty of this approach is that it leverages the incumbent's advantages against the incumbent. In political terms, these are called "referendum" elections. No one knows the name or positions of the challenger. Everyone knows the incumbent.

In a referendum election, the question shifts from a choice between a known and unknown candidate to a referendum on whether to keep or replace a known incumbent. Add to the mix the refusal of the known incumbent to defend the incumbent's record, and the political scales can start to turn.

One last tactic involves shifting the burden of proof for the incumbent. Typically, incumbents, with all the perks of incumbency, enjoy the presumption that they should be allowed to continue in office. However, incumbents who refuse to answer to voters or endure the scrutiny associated with service can lose that advantage.

If an anti-incumbency mood pervades or genuine questions surround the incumbent, the refusal to even appear for a debate can be damaging. Indeed, it could be damaging enough that the election burden shifts. Instead of most voters needing a good reason to remove the incumbent, voters start needing a good reason to let the incumbent stay—especially in change elections.

Incumbents who refuse to even appear lose the ability to fulfill that burden without spending a lot of their resources doing so. In this way, political debate, even without a debate, can serve to level the election playing field.

When there is a political debate, of course, the candidates are on a level playing field. That is the goal, and challengers should plan for it.

Challengers who never really expect to get a debate rarely do. Challengers who act in every respect, including debate preparation and proposed rules, as if they expect to debate often do (unexpectedly in some cases). Challengers should never be the dog that caught the bus. Instead, from day one, challengers and their campaigns should be prepared for the reality that a debate will happen.

With each step outlined, the likelihood increases that the challenger ends up on the stage with the incumbent they want to beat. Unfortunately, too often, they are not ready when that happens.

After all, today's social media world, with cable news and the internet, operates as virtual megaphones for creating enough noise that an incumbent or frontrunner can no longer refuse to appear for a debate. But there still may be some incumbents that need a little extra push. When that happens, one more option exists. In the modern political world of mobile phones with video/audio recording, challengers, with help of zealous supporters, can now force opponents to confront questions even without a debate.

Every encounter with a reporter, aggressive supporter,

political activist, or just random meeting can now be recorded and go viral. The only safe places for candidates not ready for the unexpected are to go into hiding or not show up for a debate. At least with a debate, the candidate can prepare and rely on the rules. In most respects, it is probably safer to be in a debate with rules than virtually anywhere else on the campaign trail.

If an incumbent simply decides to go into hiding (lockdown), challengers have the option of contests or missing person's postings with prizes for finding the incumbent. These efforts often have a surprising rate of success. The tough part is weathering the initial ridicule to reach the point where the efforts evolve from silly to serious.

With all these tools and more at the disposal of challengers, the decision to simply avoid debates or not debate is no longer the "no brainer" it was before. This is especially the case in the context of competitive primaries.

Hotly-contested primaries with lots of candidates have taken a blanket refusal to debate off the table for everyone other than prohibitive favorites. Especially in jurisdictions in which a plurality wins, the risks are simply too great for any candidate to sit out the debates in a multi-candidate primary or election.

Oddly enough, most incumbents and frontrunners actually do much better in formal political debates than challengers seeking a new job. After all, there is a reason they are the incumbent or frontrunner.

First, incumbents routinely encounter the issues and participate in debates in the performance of their jobs—from county commissioner to United States Senate. If practice makes perfect, incumbents should be pretty good. Certainly, they are much more practiced than most challengers.

More significantly, they are typically much more versed in the issues than most challengers. Most have been briefed or prepped more often on the issues associated with their job than challengers new to the stage. So, incumbents have much less to fear from political debates than most believe. Indeed, they often carry with them onto the stage some of the perks of incumbency.

No matter how much the moderator or the media attempt to level the playing field, an incumbent has the advantage when they walk out on the stage. It is reflected in their body language, their words, and their appearance. In fact, there have even been debates where the voters decided who was more prepared to serve by the way a candidate walked out for introductions.

Make no mistake, political debates are still risky business. But challenges to political debates can no longer be completely ignored in hopes that a challenger can never catch up. The ultimate decision will greatly depend on the individual facts and circumstances of each election contest and the candidates. Increasingly, as mass communication becomes more commonplace, the choice will become more and more difficult.

Eventually, with each passing election cycle, voters' expectations and the realities of modern political campaigns will start to make both candidates' decisions for them. If not already, debates will become a seemingly inevitable part of every campaign.

CHAPTER 6

LOGISTICS

These seemingly simple questions have complicated answers dictated by the circumstances of every election contest. Who could have imagined there would be twenty debates(!) for the Republican nomination for the United States presidential election in 2012? In 2016, the Democratic presidential nomination debates easily surpassed that number. In upcoming elections, especially those with ten-plus candidates, the total number of debates could easily grow even more.

Of course, not every election year involves a presidential election or engenders anywhere close to the same level of interest. But as the appetite of cable news, social media, and, more importantly, voters' interest continues to grow, the number of likely debates will undoubtedly follow.

Admittedly, some part of this demand is the insatiable appetite of television for content. Political debates have become the latest televised sport of choice for many, and many candidates eager for content are more than willing to participate.

With no legal limit on the number of debates and an insatiable appetite for political contests, the number of debates is only limited by the candidates themselves or the political parties. Although the most visible parties regulating political debate have been the national political parties, there is no reason that state and local political parties cannot do so as well.

Indeed, there are good reasons for political parties to assume the onus of setting the boundaries for political debates in the selection of their nominees for public office. Rather than force individual candidates to take the heat for limits (that could be unpopular), political parties can "provide cover" and do so with relative impunity.

Obviously, rules designed to favor a single political candidate or otherwise dictate the outcome can delegitimize the entire nomination process. But, in absence of such an obvious abuse, political parties have largely free reign in setting the rules for political debates.

In the abstract, the goal of any political party should be to nominate the candidate with the best chances of winning the general election. Unfortunately, it is not that easy. Most political parties are filled with activists loyal to a particular candidate, leader, or faction. Not surprisingly, those same activists often favor rules that benefit their candidate or group the most—regardless of whether that produces the candidate most likely to win the general election.

Behind the scenes in the GOP presidential nomination process, open war often broke out with never-Trumpers attempting repeatedly to keep President Trump from winning the nomination. This included heated and bitterly contested decisions aimed at limiting or precluding his participation at the political debates.

In the end, the only debate that President Trump missed was a debate he chose to skip. As it turned out, he ended up winning the nomination and then the general election. But his continued participation was nowhere near as easy as it may have appeared at the time.

One thing that the RNC Subcommittee on Debates learned over the course of the 2012 and 2016 election cycles was that cable news outlets wanted, indeed *needed*, the political debates much more than the candidates did. Not only were the debates instant entertainment content, but they were also a hit by cable news standards.

As a result, cable news organizations continuously increased their outlays for sets, extras, promotions, and even promos as part of the package to convince the RNC to award them a debate. And they were rewarded with ratings that translated into lots of viewers—leading up to the debate, during the debate, and after the debate.

From 2012, when former Speaker Newt Gingrich conflated civic responsibility with competitive political entertainment through President Trump's charisma attracting viewers by the millions, political debates started to drive the demand for more political debates.

There is a good lesson in this transformation of political debate from a boring set of political speeches to verbal combat with associated theatrics. To be truly effective, political debates must be entertaining. If candidates and political parties want voters to watch, they must give them a reason to watch. In this sense, entertaining the voters is a prerequisite to educating voters.

Of course, notwithstanding the important role political debates can now play in the outcome of an election, it is important to remember that no candidate has to participate in a political debate. Senator Mitt Romney proved that in 2012 when, after winning the Florida GOP presidential primary, he abruptly refused to participate in any more debates.

The other two candidates in the race at the time, Speaker Newt Gingrich and Senator Rick Santorum, could debate all they wanted, but these events lacked the same legitimacy as a "true GOP presidential debate" without the frontrunner, Senator Romney, participating.

Senator Romney knew it, the cable news networks knew it, and the other candidates knew it. And so, with his refusal to participate in any more debates, that potential impact of future debates was neutered.

So, if one candidate sees the margin grow to a virtually insurmountable lead, there is a strategic value in refusing to participate in more debates. After all, refusing to show up for a previously agreed debate does not remove a candidate's name from the ballot. It may not garner good press in the short term, but it is not disqualifying.

Similarly, if a favorite sees a challenger move ahead in the polls, then the candidate and the campaigns may want more debates to regain momentum and the lead. Or, if something unexpected happens, there is no more effective tool to deal with it than to tackle it head-on in a debate with the opponent there.

As these examples illustrate, there is no absolute answer for how many debates are the right number, and the answer may change during the course of the election. To state the obvious, the best answer to "how many" is to debate enough to win—whether it is one or twenty or (most likely) somewhere in between.

The key is to consciously plan for political debate as part of the campaign strategy and engage in debates as often or as little as the strategy dictates. As with every other aspect of a campaign, adapt to the ebbs and flows of the election using the advantages of political debate in the process.

One important factor in deciding "how many" is just how comfortable the candidate is debating. If the candidate is a natural, taking little time for preparation and advancing the overall campaign strategy with each performance, then debate early and often.

On the other hand, if the candidate requires excessive preparation (taking valuable time away from campaigning and fundraising), is not very good (losing ground with each debate), and simply hates debating, then limit the number of debates to those which are absolutely necessary. The key is that the debates should advance the campaign's objective of winning.

Debates should never be scheduled just for the sake of having done them. It is worth noting that debate skills— like nearly every other form of communication skills—can be improved with proper instruction and practice. It has never been true that "practice makes perfect," but receiving guidance from a debate coach and practicing can help any candidate perform better.

Interestingly, the "when" and the "where" dictate the "how many." If the election involves a relatively low-profile race and the proposed debates are just days away from the election, then the number will be small due to the limits of the calendar.

On the other hand, if debates begin long before qualifying (like the 2012 GOP presidential and 2016 Democratic presidential debates), expect them to continue on and on through the primary election and likely through the general election.

The "where" really depends on the amount of media coverage and the rules for determining who can attend. If the media coverage is universal (like a presidential debate), then the location matters little. When that occurs, make sure the candidate's supporters get tickets and can sit in the audience.

The idea of a neutral or quiet audience is whimsical. Since

golf fans began cheering loudly at the Ryder Cup, obedient silent audiences who never make a sound after being so instructed simply do not exist.

If there are no pre-agreed allocations of tickets or other measures to assure a balanced audience, it is political malpractice to not stack the audience. There is a reason "home-field advantage" matters. Candidates, like sports teams, should take advantage of it.

When the audience weighs in, things (for an assortment of reasons) tend to go better than when the audience does not. As a result, if the seats are up for grabs, make sure the candidate's supporters get there earlier, take up a seat (starting with the closest row first), and do their job—support their candidate.

This dynamic can throw an opponent off, keep the candidate on message, and police the moderator. One perfect example is the 2012 South Carolina GOP presidential debate where Speaker Newt Gingrich verbally "body slammed" CNN moderator John King.

That debate and the corresponding South Carolina presidential preference primary was over within five minutes of the beginning of the debate once the crowd rallied around Speaker Gingrich. None of the other candidates could recover, and Speaker Gingrich went on to win the South Carolina GOP presidential primary. Stacking the audience, when possible, can also help bolster the confidence of candidates who need a boost.

Indeed, it is so powerful that some campaigns go so far as to orchestrate the audience with floor leaders and signals (or, in today's world—texts or emails), telling attendees when to cheer, jeer, or just be silent. No candidate should allow this to happen when it can be prevented with good campaign groundwork.

Several tools exist for preventing an opponent from stacking the audience. First and foremost, make sure the candidate's supporters are ready, willing, and able to take any and all seats up for grabs at the earliest possible moment and then do it. If both sides are doing their jobs, very few seats will be up for grabs, preventing the possibility altogether.

Another option is to have no audience. Unfortunately, debates without audiences tend to have much less zest or zeal and make for bad entertainment. Bad debates with no emotion and no urgency, absent a real gaffe by one candidate or the other, typically do little to move the needle in an election contest.

But that could be a candidate's goal. Debates without audiences tend to drift toward lifelessness, making for bad television and little interest. For an incumbent or favorite forced to debate, this could be exactly what the doctor ordered. The candidate gets credit for debating, but no one watches or cares, meaning the challenger gains little from the effort.

Another option is to require tickets, with each side receiving an equal number of tickets. Obviously, if one candidate or the other fails to attract folks to attend the debate, this accomplishes little if the other candidate fills the place up.

Some sponsoring organizations want to sell the tickets. Without addressing all of the campaign finance law issues implicated, selling tickets does not do much to mitigate against a hostile audience. Worse yet, it often diverts contributions from the campaigns to an organization that often has an agenda of its own.

In the real world, the audience is an important part of the

debate. Virtually every attendee at a debate will have already made their mind up before the debate begins. If there are any undecided voters with nothing better to do than go to a political debate (how many people who aren't sports fans attend sporting events?), the chances are they will remain undecided by the end of the debate.

Therefore, recognize the audience for what it is—an opportunity to have supporters to show their support. Either neutralize it by making sure that the candidate has as many in the audience as the opponent or use it as evidence of support the candidate has but their opponent does not.

Within all this context comes the issue of "where" the debate takes place. It is much easier to get attendees in areas where the candidate has great support than in places where there is little support. With this in mind, locations in areas of great support or neutral territory are much better than locations with little support.

This dynamic of location extends beyond just attendees at the debate. It also extends to media coverage, social media reaction, and the follow-up to the debate. It is the reason the "where" makes the top three list for issues to control in scheduling debates.

Importantly, the "how many, when, and where" issues do not happen in a vacuum. There are a multitude of factors that can impact the decision-making.

Candidates desperate for a debate with a favorite expanding a lead may leave little choice but to accept a single late debate in a bad area. Sometimes a "Hail Mary" is not only the best shot a candidate has, but it may be the only shot (and sometimes a "Hail Mary" works, and the underdog wins against the odds).

But, if given a choice, opt for (1) the number of debates that do not spread the campaign (or the candidate) too thin, (2) in relatively close proximity to election day, and, (3) in an at least neutral (if not favorable) venue backed by a solid base of supporters willing to show up and do their part.

The 2020 election season will be very interesting, with the likely inclusion of debates taking place in a fully online environment, in which there will be no audience in the room with the candidates but potentially far more streaming the event live than otherwise would have attended.

Applying the aforementioned guidelines to the virtual format, candidates should be sure to negotiate that the comments sections be turned off (it's vital that the candidates themselves maintain the attention of the audience during the debate), and the campaign team should work even harder to get supporters to follow along online and share their positive reactions to the debate on their social media.

CHAPTER 7

CANDIDATE PARTICIPATION

Like the other questions, this question—who participates —sounds easy enough with an apparently simple answer— the candidates, of course. Yet, like all the other details of competitive political debate at the highest level, there are no easy answers. Instead, finding the right answers for winning requires the discipline to drill down on the even the most basic questions.

Even starting with the easy answer—the candidates are participants in the debate—is complicated enough. What exactly does that mean? Does every candidate who pays the qualifying fee (or files a pauper affidavit) automatically get a spot on the political debate stage? Of course not.

Even with the Republican presidential primary debates of 2012 and the Democratic presidential primary debates of 2016 having stages overflowing with candidates, neither party included *every* possible candidate in debates. Not all candidates are created equal when it comes to winning at political debate.

And pointedly, nothing mandates that the rules for political debate must be fair and balanced. What is clear is that to be more than just an argument, there must be rules. And there is no rule more outcome determinative between winners and losers than those rules that dictate who gets to participate. Like the lottery, one cannot win if they are not playing.

Hence, the rules about participation are the most fiercely-fought and jealously-guarded rules of political debate. To make the point, the Commission on Presidential Debates Rules have allowed only one "third candidate" to participate in presidential and vice presidential debates. It is the gatekeeper of all other rules when it comes to political debates.

At the presidential and vice presidential level, the limit on "who" can participate in presidential election debates has a name. In 2000, Green Party nominee Ralph Nader dubbed it the political "Khyber Pass." With television increasing publicity and third-party candidates following the 1960 Kennedy-Nixon presidential debates steadily building a case for more candidates on the stage, the main political parties increased their influence over the process.

The Democratic and Republican national parties seized control of the political debate process for presidential elections by creating the Commission on Presidential Debates in 1987. With the two major political parties backing the Commission, it became virtually impossible for any candidate other than the major party nominees to make the stage and have a shot at a win in the general election.

Since the Commission on Debates firmly established its control over the rules in 1987, only one third-party candidate —Ross Perot in 1992—has participated in a presidential general election debate. Even then, it was the two candidates, President George H. W. Bush and President Bill Clinton, that overruled the Commission, thus permitting Ross Perot (and his running mate Admiral James Stockdale) to participate in the debates.

Interestingly, both did so for strategic reasons, each believing Perot's participation would help their campaign when Perot drew more voters from their opponent than them. Political scientists continue to debate whether Perot's third party played a deciding factor in the 1992 election. His candidacy certainly affected the presidential debates, forcing a change from the traditional one-on-one format.

Since 2000, the Commission has staunchly stuck to two main eligibility criteria for participation. First, to be eligible for the presidential general election debate, a candidate's name must appear on enough state ballots to capture the requisite 270 Electoral College votes to win in the general election. Second, to participate, a candidate must reach a threshold of 15% support among voters in five national polls leading up to the debate.

The Commission takes these limits so seriously that the Commission had Green Party nominee Ralph Nader barred from the debates between President George W. Bush and Vice President Albert Gore in 2000. In 2012, Jill Stein (and her running mate Cheri Honkala) were arrested for attempting to attend the debate at Hofstra University when President Barack Obama debated Senator Mitt Romney.

While the rules governing participation by candidates are the most significant and dominate the pre-debate strategizing, the Commission on Presidential Debates, as well as all other groups governing or shaping debate rules, do not limit themselves to only those two topics.

Entire books, articles, and news programs are devoted to everything from the height of podiums to whether candidates can have a glass of water during the debate. So, the theme for winning elections using political debates remains the same— rules matter and the candidate that can best shape or dictate the rules helps that candidate to win.

Whether the big topics, like the decision of whether to agree or refuse to allow other candidates to participate in a political debate, or the little ones, like whether to allow notepads on the podium, the combination of the political debate rules influence who will be in the best position to win before the first word is uttered in the debate.

For candidates and the campaign staff, decisions regarding debate rules should be calculated ones. Consider the impact on winning the election by looking at the numbers and determining whether any given rule helps or hurts, always recognizing that some aspects (e.g., who gets on the stage) matter a lot more than others (e.g., breaks during the debate).

In some respects, the "who" gets decided by the process. For example, in most general election contests, political party rules decide who the parties' nominees will be on the general election debate. On the other hand, in states or jurisdictions with "jungle primaries" (a primary where the two top vote getters make the runoff even if from the same political party) that may not be the case.

Increasingly, as social media and cable programming make access to voters easier and easier, candidates and campaigns can expect a tiered process. First, there will be multi-candidate primary contests. Some will have a runoff for the party nomination. Once the parties' nominees are selected, they will face off in a general election debate (and even those can, in rare circumstances, involve one more run-off election with a corresponding final debate).

While one part of this book may seem inapplicable due to the rules of a particular state or jurisdiction, it may become directly relevant to a different part of the process. The point is that as the format, participants, sequencing, etc., change from debate to debate (for whatever reason), certain guidelines become directly applicable for participating in those kinds of debates.

To deal with the rules for participation as part of the overall rules package for modern political debates, political parties, news outlets, civic groups, campaigns and candidates have, like the Commission on Presidential Debates, turned to the establishment of criteria. The candidate must be represented in any discussion in which the criteria, like all other rules, are being created. Then, the key is to advocate for those that favor the candidate.

Crowded fields can be whittled down by using eligibility criteria for making the debate cut—restricting the field of viable candidates before a single election contest has been decided. Look at how many Democrats dropped out of the 2020 Democratic presidential nomination process before the first caucus or primary was even held. The reverse is also true.

Moving up from the junior stage in the 2012 GOP presidential debates propelled Senator Rick Santorum from a long shot to a finalist with eventual nominee Senator Mitt Romney and Speaker Newt Gingrich. Consequently, from the outset, candidates must develop and implement an effective strategy for meeting the criteria for participation in the political debates.

Effective strategies will have to consider factors beyond the control of any one candidate, such as the number of candidates and the level of input that each candidate has in developing the criteria. Primaries with candidates numbering in the double digits will inevitably involve some combination of polling, fundraising, and measurable support.

It is critical that once the criteria are set, meeting the criteria becomes an important focus of the candidate and the campaign. Being on the stage is a force-multiplier on nearly every other part of the campaign strategy. As Ralph Nader despairingly noted of his exclusion from the 2000 presidential debates, even though he often drew large crowds, "in one debate I would have reached more people, by 50-fold, than I reached by filling all the major arenas."

Making the cut matters in election contests. If the criteria do in fact include metrics such as fundraising, polling (local and national), or other objectively measurable factors, design a part of the campaign plan that focuses solely on meeting the criteria.

Being close is not good enough. Candidates either meet the criteria or they do not. Because it is binary, the consequences of just missing the cut by a little or a lot is the same: disastrous. So, do not miss the cut even if it means writing a check to the campaign or spending more time in friendly areas to drive polls up.

Making the cut is so important that every critical date should be carefully calendared for measuring the status of the campaign against each of the objective criteria for being on the political debate stage. These little details are very important.

For years, few candidates or campaigns rarely gave much thought about the "who," leaving such determinations to others, such as the media, other candidates, or political parties. Yet, there are plenty of opportunities to influence the criteria used for determining who gets on stage and even where they stand.

There are multiple players attempting to control the game, and the leverage each has is greatly influenced by the real power of the voters. When viewers tuned in to watch the early debates by the millions, cable news networks noticed and offered more and more to get sponsorship of a debate.

In 2012, the Republican National Committee set the precedent for political parties taking control of debates.

Behind closed doors, the RNC and its Debate Subcommittee really did not know what they had. With each passing debate, RNC Chair Priebus and those who worked within the media did. By the end of the debates, the RNC had more control than anyone, even the candidates themselves.

In contrast, President Trump demonstrated he could skip a debate and still survive. Senator Romney proved he could marginalize (and effectively end) future debates by refusing to participate when the number of viable candidates reached three.

When President Trump realized he was the top draw for a debate, he realized he could shove a network and host out by refusing to participate. When Senator Romney's campaign figured out that Senator Santorum and Speaker Gingrich needed the resources generated by debates and there was little interest in a debate between those in second and third, his refusal to participate was the end of debates in 2012.

The bottom line is to play the cards the candidate and campaign are dealt to optimize the debate dynamics (especially the "who" that gives the candidate the best chances for moving up and eventually winning). Understand that while a political party, media outlet, or candidate(s) might seemingly have most of the control, manipulating the voter/viewer dynamic is the single most effective technique for pushing rules that help and vetoing those that don't.

The power to make decisions about the criteria for participating in a political debate can never be ignored or forfeited to someone else. One of the worst mistakes for a candidate or campaign is to allow someone else to have unfettered control of the debate rules.

President Ronald Reagan understood this in 1980. Republicans did not understand it in 2012. Now, both national political parties know it well, and state and local parties are beginning to understand it.

In this modern new world of political debate and the associated rules, there is much talk of fairness, openness, transparency, and equal opportunities. However, most of this talk is disconnected from reality. Instead, those deciding the criteria for making and remaining on the debate stage are engaging in raw, bare-knuckled politics creating winners and making losers.

This is true whether it is a political party, media outlet, or the candidates themselves. Having someone on the inside of that decision-making group is essential.

Candidates who want to live to campaign and debate another day, and those advising them must understand this simple political fact. Only then can they have any realistic hope of advancing effective, meaningful strategies for making the rules work for them rather than falling victim to rules designed to eliminate them.

The system will inevitably work to the advantage of front-runners, political insiders, fundraising bundlers, and media executives unless it is counterbalanced. When these forces are working together, they are virtually unstoppable.

Consider the Commission on Presidential Debates. The national political parties want to limit the universe of candidates to two—either a Republican or a Democrat. Television networks know that while entertaining at the front end of the nomination process, having more than two candidates at the back end for the election process is just too complicated. The media wants a political Super Bowl, which means only two teams on the field.

This means that for lesser-known candidates, or those

attempting to just break through, more risks must be taken to crack the glass ceilings that stand in the way of their continued progression toward continued participation. However, irrational risks with no target in mind are never a good idea.

The key is calculated risk. But make no mistake, the essence of "breaking" through is "breakage"—forcing the current systems in place backed by institutional barriers (walls and ceilings) perpetuated by established power brokers prepared to do everything to retain control. Oddly, success at breaking the mold will (as Speaker Gingrich proved in 1994) bring them back into the new fold, as political activists are never far from those in power.

Oddly, success at getting a little limelight is more commonplace than most pundits believe. It is almost a revolving door, allowing voters to see almost every candidate somewhere near frontrunner status. And, on cue, most stumble. This is an important feature in the American system. Most get a chance at the center of the stage to prove their mettle.

With history as a judge, many shooting stars fall just as fast as they rose. And the higher a candidate climbs, the further the candidate can fall. In the context of political debate, increasing the chances of winning the election means just one thing—survival. Every debate that a candidate stays on the stage for, with other candidates dropping off, the chances for winning on Election Day go up.

There are two easy ways to lose a political debate: losing before ever getting on stage by not doing the brass tacks of what it takes to meet the criteria or losing on the stage by failing to perform. Winners avoid both.

CHAPTER 8

THE MODERATORS / PANELISTS

It is possible to have a moderator-less debate. President Abraham Lincoln and Senator Stephen Douglas proved it. But, while a referee-less football game is possible at some level, referees are increasingly indispensable (now including instant video replay). Modern debates even have instant fact-checkers whispering information into the ear of the moderator, for credibility, as a fair process—even for debates.

Just like umpires make the difference in the outcome of a baseball game, moderators can influence the outcome of a political debate (and like umpires/referees, the audience complains about them but frequently depend on them to understand what's happening).

Thus, while a moderator-less debate may be tempting, it is wiser to focus on ensuring proper moderation of the debate instead. The RNC Rules Committee proved that, over the course of a nomination process, fair debates are within reach —if candidates with sponsors and political parties exercise the correct oversight with voters as the ultimate check.

Monitoring the monitor is fraught with all the challenges of setting the criteria for participating in a debate. All of the same institutional pitfalls exist for debate monitor oversight —from selection to review to post-debate commentary.

Campaigns must take all the same precautions in making sure that the candidates are as involved with the role and oversight of monitors as they are with debate criteria. What should candidates and consultants watch for and insist upon? The starting point must inevitably be identifying the role of the monitor.

With rules as the essence of debate (as opposed to argument), one of the most important roles for a moderator is enforcement (to the extent possible) of the very rules that make it a debate, and gaining compliance is no easy thing. Indeed, some of the more recent "debates" appear to be little more than an opening separated from a closing with almost non-stop talking over each other.

It is one reason that more recent debates tend to move the political needle so little. Increasingly, many political debates are gravitating closer to the cacophony of cable news talk shows (complete with commercial breaks) than events intended to inform and influence voters.

With this steady drift towards verbal free-for-all, the importance of moderators has never been greater. On the flip side, with greater roles to play, the moderators' influence over the outcome only increases. Similar to the behavior of some of the umpires and referees in sports, this is because the moderators themselves increasing seek the same level of celebrity as the candidates.

But while the best officiated games are the ones in which no one knows the names of the referees or umpires, that same standard has little chance of success in modern televised political debate. Consequently, oversight by the candidates and political parties has become even more important as the entertainment value of political debates has increased.

In sports, referees and umpires are also reviewed for performance. The purpose of both the leagues and the referees/umpires is to get better and use the review to select the best for even bigger sporting events. Evaluation criteria notably do not include outshining the players as the stars of the sporting event.

Like referees/umpires, moderators do have very important roles to play.

Generally, these roles can be divided into two categories: the technical and the substantive. Both roles help facilitate a successful political debate, regardless of whether viewed from vantage point of the incumbent/frontrunner (protective of a lead) or a challenger (trying to catch up) or even a network (looking for viewers and credibility in the political commentary context).

From a technical standpoint, the moderator has the ultimate responsibility for enforcing the rules to which the candidates and others have agreed. This role has become increasingly difficult as candidates have become seemingly oblivious to the rules with virtual impunity (a tactic addressed later in this book).

Moderators, with the support of the media and sponsors, still have the tools to enforce rules. After all, they do control the microphone, the camera, and to some extent the audience. At some point, effective moderators can direct that the microphone be turned off, the camera pointed away or cut to a commercial break, or solicit the audience to action with the red light indicating time is up.

Moderators cannot use these tools with impunity themselves. Candidates, campaigns, audiences, and viewers will hold moderators to a serious standard of fairness and evenhandedness. And, when that line gets crossed, it can be the moderator that gets the hook or wrath of even others in the media (especially those eager to make their case for consideration as a future moderator).

In the modern political debate context, the moderator's role still includes enforcing the rules regarding which candidate goes first and last, how long each candidate gets to speak, and, more importantly, who gets to offer a rebuttal to another candidate's attack. And there are some rules that are not candidate-specific, such as how long the debate will last, when to take commercial breaks, and when the time has come for the last question.

In the abstract, these rules would seem to be harmless; however, like an official's commercial timeout dictated by the network during an important last drive in a football game, they can impact the outcome of the contest. The most essential part of this technical rule's enforcement must always be objectively fair. The rule is enforced dispassionately based on objectively confirmable data (like time), regardless of who the rule enforcement helps or hurts.

With the ever-expanding role of the "entertainment" component in modern political debates, the technical rules enforcement has often been overlooked. Yet, it has never been more important. This also means that oversight of technical rules enforcement has also never been important.

In the first televised presidential debate in 1960, the even distribution of questions and time was monitored to the second. When the stakes are that high, the stakes demand such a level of technical oversight.

In today's world, the moderators' roles have evolved beyond just keeping time and alternating questioners and calling on candidates for their openings and closings. As noted earlier, everyone—candidates, campaigns, political parties, and networks—want entertainment. All want to reach as many voters as possible, even if for completely different reasons.

Clearly, there is no better way to reach voters than with an entertaining debate filled with some competitive exchanges (often considered "controversy," even if they are more like simple disagreements spiced up with some well-rehearsed one-liners).

Regulating eager candidates amidst larger audiences with the corresponding complications of modern media, even if limited to modern social media, can be tricky. Like losing sports teams that complain about the calls, there will always be allegations by candidates of favoritism, mistakes, and outright bias. Nonetheless, it is a job that must be done.

The overriding principle is to make sure that the debate is fair and impartial—ensuring each candidate has the equal opportunity to make their case to voters, which means being seen and heard without undue favoritism to either. This starts with the moderator who, after the candidates, will be the most central figure in the debate.

Make no mistake—moderators, like referees and umpires, can make a world of difference in the outcome of a political debate and the election to follow. One good example would be CNN chief political news correspondent Candy Crowley in the 2012 presidential debate between President (and Democratic presidential nominee) Barack Obama and GOP presidential nominee Senator Mitt Romney.

The topic of the townhall-style debate at Hofstra University was foreign policy, and most of the questions were on topic. In what surprised many, Senator Romney appeared to avoid sharp contrasts with President Obama on most topics. But there were differences.

Crowley had made it clear in the weeks and days leading up to the debate that she would inject herself forcefully into the debate. That should have been an early warning sign that a problem was coming.

At one point, Senator Romney sharpened his attacks, citing President Obama's allegedly changing explanations for the violence directed at State Department facilities in Benghazi, Libya, and alleging that, "for fourteen days he refused to call it an act of terror."

Although he had to know the issue was coming, President Obama's response was a tepid admonition for Senator Romney to check the transcript, suggesting that the transcript confirmed that his Administration had called the attacks on the U.S. Consulate an act of terror.

Clearly, the moment demanded fact-checking, which both political campaigns were busily doing (or had done) in preparation for the post-debate spin rooms and follow-up media coverage. Yet, moderator Crowley stepped in with what appeared to be "real-time fact-checking" by a purportedly disinterested third party.

Before more could be said, Crowley intervened and directed her response directly to Senator Romney. Crowley and said, "He did in fact, sir." The impact was real and important. Senator Romney knew that Crowley had a host of researchers back in the studio feeding her information, so it undoubtedly made him less sure of his response. In the eyes of viewers, it cast some doubt as to his credibility.

By interjecting to make a "ruling" on which candidate was telling the truth, Candy Crowley violated what should be the rule against moderators participating in the debate on the merits. Her other behavior throughout the debate—interrupting the candidates and cutting off exchanges even when the candidates wanted to continue—extended the moderator's influence over the debate beyond the traditionally acceptable boundaries.

Rather than simply leave it up to the candidates (and after the debate their campaigns) to correct misstatements or exaggerations, moderator Candy Crowley, with the assistance of her network CNN through her earpiece, assumed that role during the debate itself. And, as it turned out, at least on the timing of when the President claimed he spoke the words, she was wrong. The debate over the details proves why her interjection was out of line.

The Benghazi attack occurred on September 11, with Senator Romney alleging President Obama waited fourteen days to call it an "act of terror." The President responded—and Crowley falsely confirmed—that it was only one day later in his Rose Garden remarks on September 12.

Analysis of the debate in *Foreign Policy* identified a campaign event in Colorado on September 13 as the first time the President directly referenced the event as an act of terror—an argument over these distinctions hardly rose to the level of a moment for the moderator needing to "make a ruling" as Crowley did.

Unfortunately, in recent years, this pattern of moderator-centric debates has become an increasingly frequent event, with moderators competing with candidates for airtime, credibility, and name recognition. Perceptions of unfairness and allegations of outright bias can lead to candidates refusing to participate, as when President Trump boycotted a Fox News debate moderated by Megyn Kelly.

Candidates are not the only ones who can react forcefully to moderators who are believed to have crossed this line. During the 2016 GOP presidential debates, the Republican National Committee Debate Committee cancelled NBC's right to host the GOP debate after it reached the conclusion that the network was deliberately misusing its sponsorship and moderator to undermine all the GOP candidates, necessarily including the eventual nominee.

It is critically important for candidates and political parties to take appropriate measures to protect themselves from moderators and sponsors. The goal is to make sure that the moderator will be impartial and fair (while the candidates attempt to tilt the debate in their favor by leveraging the rules in ways that benefit them most).

Most importantly, candidates and political parties should fully limit to the maximum extent possible the ability of a moderator to become a participant in the debate. Moderators should be the enforcers of the objective rules and otherwise facilitators of debate—nothing more.

The debate is not about the moderators, for their career advancement or an event to be manipulated by them. Candidates must assume the responsibility for preventing that from happening.

Sometimes, these issues extend beyond the moderators to include others, such as a panel of questioners (often news or political reporters) charged with the responsibility of posing the questions to the candidates. These same challenges can extend to them, as they too can be tempted to seize the spotlight for their own purposes rather than facilitate a political debate among candidates trying to win an election.

Some candidates have suggested, unrealistically, the possibility of simply leaving the debate once it becomes clear that it will not be a fair one. That is never a good idea; once the debate has started, it is too late. Most voters conclude from such unexpected departures that candidates who cannot handle to heat of a hostile moderator or panelist probably cannot handle the pressures of elected public office.

Good solutions do exist for managing moderators and panelists. First, some responsibilities can be subject to immediate
transparency, outsourced to others jointly designated by the
campaigns or, better yet, both.

One of the smartest moves most airlines made at their
gates was to publicly display the upgrade list and the cleared
list for everyone to see. Once everyone could see the order
of the names and confirm for themselves that nothing was
amiss, the whispers of favoritism by gate agents rigging the
lists seemed to dissipate.

Similarly, when the candidates, audience, and viewers can
see the clock and the corresponding yellow and red lights,
fewer questions remain about whether each candidate is
complying with the same time limits. Everyone, including
the candidates, can see the time. It is why transparency is so
effective in making sure rules are equally applied.

Of course, there is also no good reason why a moderator
should keep time during a debate—it unnecessarily adds to
their responsibilities. In most sports, the timekeeper is distinct
from the referee, and the one sport—soccer—where the head
referee is also the timekeeper has the most complaints about
unfair timekeeping.

Have a timekeeper jointly selected by the candidates or
each candidate could designate someone to also keep time.
Audits in real time can prevent a timekeeper from giving one
candidate more time than the other.

As reflected in the rules for the presidential debates, and
effectively detailed in *Kennedy vs. Nixon*, there are a litany
of ways to inject transparency and accountability into the
objectively measurable components of a political debate. These
can include the number of questions, face time on camera, the
right to rebuttal, etc.

Sometimes, there may be occasions where such accountability is not possible in real time during the debate. When
that happens, there is no reason for the same mistake to
be made twice. If a moderator, questioner, timekeeper, etc.,
cannot be fair and impartial, then take steps to make sure
they do not participate in any future debates, whether in the
same cycle or future cycles.

But there are many ways to create the objectivity necessary
for accountability before the debate ever begins. So, to maximize this accountability, candidates and their campaigns
should try to make as many things as possible objectively
measurable.

It is not that difficult. Some of the most obvious possibilities include:

> Order of openings
> Length of openings
> Sequence of questions
> Topics of the debate
> Length of answers
> Length of rebuttals
> Order of closings
> Length of closings
> Breaks
> Length of the debate

Of course, the list does not stop there. If the debates are
televised, the direction of the camera, the amount of face
time, and breaks can be addressed. If audiences attend, then
the rules regarding audience conduct (and the remedies for
misconduct) can be addressed.

The more objectively measurable the rule is, like the

amount of time for an opening, the greater the ability to enforce it. Two notable traps to avoid are as follows.

First, any suggestion of permitting each candidate to designate a questioner is a bad idea. No matter how well prepared, a candidate will not fare well from the cross-examination of a well-trained trial lawyer appointed by their opponent. And while their appointee might be helpful, it can never overcome the harm done by a skillful questioner.

Second, suggestions that the candidates simply question each other never works out well. In most cases, it devolves into an argument without rules (which is why moderators, despite their flaws, are needed). Regardless, the debate will inevitably turn inordinately personal bringing out the worst in both candidates no matter how committed either is to stay on the high ground.

"When they go low, we go high" sounds good in the abstract; the problem is that it never works very well in debates. Rather than test it with an election on the line, the better option is to agree on the rules so that the debates focus on the issues and the candidates can decide where to go from there. This means impartial moderators and questioners, focused on facilitating discourse and exploring meaningful issues.

In the end, the subjective component for measuring moderators and panelists depends on good research, past performance, and meaningful evaluation of both historical and recent work. Many potential moderators and panelists are well known by all the candidates and political operatives. For those, it is relatively easy to make a well-informed decision.

Candidates should be wary of the unknown questioners and academics. The unknown carry with them unknown risks, and unknown risks can do more damage than known ones.

With few exceptions, academics tend to be as entertaining on the debate stage as their students perceive them to be in the classroom. Worse yet, they are prone to ask questions that focus on details about which the majority of voters are not concerned, while overlooking more general-level issues about which voters want to hear.

If it is available, candidates should watch video of those selected to get a feel for their rhythm, favorite issues, and thoughts. In some situations, candidates should consider jointly meeting with the moderator to discuss the ground rules.

Doing so has the added benefit of becoming familiar with the vocal tone and speech patterns of the moderator; familiarity is an effective defense to the unknown and regulating the unpredictable.

CHAPTER 9

FORMATS FOR DEBATE

Every debate is different than every other debate. Notwith-standing the similarity of format or rules, the type of debate really does vary with the candidates, moderators, election contest, and a host of other factors.

These distinguishing characteristics do not mean that common formats have developed. And, when multiple debates are scheduled for the same election contests, it is common that sponsors and/or candidates will vary the formats.

Sometimes, the formats are dictated by the circumstances of the election contest. For example, in elections with multiple candidates, a townhall format is not feasible—having ten candidates roam around a stage would simply be unworkable.

On the other hand, when the field has narrowed to two candidates, virtually every format is on the table. When that happens, each candidate looks for the format that most favors their candidate.

For other reasons, sponsors and media outlets want variety to spike up ratings and entertainment. In assessing which is best, candidates and their teams can largely consider formats in the context of two factors: the position of their candidate on the stage and the method of responding to questions.

Less comfortable candidates often prefer more formality, which limits the amount of real-time thinking during the debate. With greater formality, a candidate can (or should be able to) predict exactly what will happen and how it will happen. All the candidate must do is deliver the content.

Candidates more comfortable in a public setting typically prefer informal settings with more opportunity for free exchanges with the audience and the other candidate(s). Charismatic candidates especially prefer the opportunity to connect with people, including both those in attendance and those who are not.

Within these boundaries, formal traditional debate rules and informal chats on stage lie opportunities for candidates and campaigns to choose the format or type of debate that best suits their objectives. For purposes of discussion, it is easiest to discuss this issue in the context of three categories of debate formats:

1. stationary standing (typically behind a podium) with regimented speaking;

2. sitting (typically behind a desk) with blended speaking limitations; and,

3. standing and moving around in a townhall-type setting with fewer, if any, limits on who speaks when and for how long.

Needless to say, the dynamics of these types of debates vary so greatly that most often the only thing they have in common is that all involve an argument with rules, i.e., technically a debate. For each of the candidates, depending on their preferences and talents, converting uncertain variables—from movement to duration, from what might happen into what will happen—is the role of rules.

It is incumbent upon candidates and campaigns to regulate their risks and effectively prepare for the risks that do remain. In that way, effectively-negotiated rules can reduce the amount of debate preparation required since there is no reason to prepare for things the rules prohibit.

In assessing which format is best, consider both what is best for the candidate AND what is worst for the opponent. Sometimes, the opponent's discomfort (and corresponding nervousness translating into unforced errors) can outweigh the candidate's preference for one format over another.

The ultimate choice, to the extent permitted, should be an informed one based on all the circumstances, not a default decision that no one discussed. Especially in political debates, no opportunity for an edge should ever be missed.

Format choice is one place where video is effective in informing decision makers. Film the candidate in each of the formats—even if just using a mobile phone—and then watch it.

Most people seeing some part of the debate will see it on television or on their computer, so the candidate and the campaign team should see what voters will see. What looks so good in person may not look so good on screen. The best way to make that determination is to view the candidate from the point of view the audience will have.

The ultimate goal should be authenticity. Unfortunately, authenticity is one of those things that does not translate so well through a camera. In those situations, the backdrop can do much to reinforce or even create it.

If the podium makes a huge difference in communicating an authoritative but likable candidate, go with a more formal debate format. If a relaxing step disconnected from the chains of a secured podium makes a candidate more appealing (or the opponent *less* appealing), then go with a townhall.

Most of all, make a decisioned choice, not a choice left to the decisions of others based on whatever objectives they may have. The differences between the kinds of debates and the impressions left with voters have been well documented in the election outcome history books. So, there is every reason to take the time to consider the choices and go with what works best.

The Podium Debate

By far, the most common political debate format involves two or more candidates standing behind podiums, responding (subject to strict time limits) to questions posed, preceded by an opening and ended with a closing. The component parts are straightforward: a podium, candidates, a moderator, potentially a panel of questioners, and maybe a timekeeper.

Regarding the podium, there is not a lot to discuss EXCEPT that all the podiums should be identical or substantially similar. If necessary, just borrow them from some local churches. No incumbent should be permitted to put the seal of their office or jurisdiction on the podium.

Podium heights can differ, just not if all adjacent to each other. Dividers (for adjacent podiums) are good since some candidates cannot resist the temptation to read what other candidates write down. Podiums should be real podiums—not desks, tables, or, as once done, a stack of boxes.

Anything else defeats the purpose of "formality." Once the decision has been made to use a podium, then the candidates should stick with all the accoutrements associated with a formal debate.

For many candidates, the podium will be the most important single item on the stage. It keeps them stable, centered, steady, and focused. It is like a safety zone, the confines of which should be a safe harbor.

It belongs to the candidate and can steady even the weakest debater all the way to the end of the debate. It can also help candidates who tend to fidget, providing them a place to calm their hands as they hold onto the podium with a hand on each corner closest to them, elbows nearly locked to ensure good posture.

Podiums are anchors, steady and solid—not buoys bobbing up and down with no signs of stability or reliability. Candidates who forget the role of the podium will lose the greatest benefit the podium brings to the debate.

While helpful, the podium should never be a crutch, a place to slouch, or a platform for pounding. Focus groups consistently show that viewers and voters do not react well to podium pounding. It is distracting and ineffective.

While pounding should be avoided, nothing prevents writing or keeping notes. Of course, this raises the question of what candidates can write on. Exactly what candidates can bring to the podium varies depending on the agreed rules.

Some allow a pen and blank pad but nothing more, while others allow a pen and pad with notes or other written reference material. In contrast, some prohibit everything except the candidate, expressly prohibiting pens, pads, props, aides, or demonstrative materials like charts or pictures.

Proponents of such a restrictive approach believe the political debate is to test the candidates, not their campaigns and certainly not their campaign literature or opposition research. Under these rules, the debate must not have any access to anything of assistance, leaving the candidates completely exposed with only intellect, speech, and knowledge to convince voters.

Few debates are so restrictive. Most permit pens and pads at the podium with which to take notes during the debate.

Beyond that, most prohibit everything else. The important thing for a candidate is to leave no doubt.

Know what the rules are regarding the use of things during the debate. If there are no rules, know it or create them. The worst outcome would be if one candidate abides by much more restrictive rules than their opponent because the rules do not prohibit it.

Finally, in podium debates, protect the candidate from the physical demands of an exceptionally long debate. If the length is inordinately long, push for stools and then make sure they are there, to avoid what happened in the 1992 presidential debate when the Clinton campaign removed the stools.

While the details regarding the other components (the moderator and/or panel of questioners, order of responses, timekeeping) are discussed in other sections, the combination of all of them does involve the intangible concept of "staging." Staging involves picturing the debate and then adjusting the picture through rules to maximize the image of a candidate.

Staging can include the order of the candidates; moving the candidates closer together or farther apart; adjusting the podiums; moving the moderators left, right, or out of view; increasing or decreasing the lighting; and so on. While the "staging" (as for a movie director) involves endless possibilities, its goal is quite simple—make the candidate look good regardless of what happens.

One final point—staging is a unique skill set that not everyone has; few campaign consultants do. They are the best at understanding the interplay between available funds, media buys, campaign rallies/events, and electioneering, but not very good at actually staging them. It is why they are campaign consultants, not movie directors (and why interior decorating is a separate profession from home construction).

Equally important, good staging necessarily depends on viewing the stage through diverse eyes. The unmistakable truth is that the lens through which people see the world, including political debates, is shaped by their own personal life.

This means their gender, race, ethnicity, religion, sexual orientation, and a host of other factors all directly impact how they see the world. It is why two different people of diverse backgrounds can look at the same photograph but see completely different things.

To replicate this phenomenon, campaigns must themselves be diverse. Absent that diversity, the candidate and the campaign will see the same thing that everyone else like them sees. But voters are diverse—at least the number of voters that a candidate needs to win an election (and that is *always* the main objective!).

Consequently, when looking at staging (as well as content), candidates and campaigns must include staff, volunteers, and consultants that are as diverse as voters are. It is the secret sauce that gives the top-tier candidates an edge over the rest.

When diversity is added to the other component parts of a podium debate, candidates and campaigns can dictate through the rules what voters, media, and others will see (and in some cases form that important first impression) before a word is spoken on the political debate stage. In many cases, it means the candidate starts the debate one step ahead.

The Seated Debate

No one knows exactly when someone suggested moving from standing behind a podium to sitting behind a desk or table. Undoubtedly, it was an intermediate step from the formal podium debate toward an "around the table" conversation.

Regardless, sitting debates are inherently awkward and make an enormous difference in virtually every aspect of a debate. If anyone has any doubts, just ask a candidate who has participated in a sitting debate.

The single most significant dynamic that makes a sitting debate challenging is physical proximity—the candidates and the moderator are inevitably seated at the same table within close physical proximity of each other. That physical proximity is fraught with risk.

It is one thing to stand next to an opponent saying bad things. It is quite another to sit next to them or across from them at a table with a moderator committed to sparking an explosion of emotions. It is why so few candidates want them and most disdain them.

The obvious exception would be candidates who have mobility impairment or other physical condition that makes standing infeasible. In these cases, expect all debates to be seated affairs, and it is crucial for the opponents of such candidates to practice in the sitting format, so as to avoid the problems noted below.

Theoretically, a conversation should permit a more reasoned or rational discussion of key issues. The problem is that the greater the intensity of the election contest, the less likely that such discussions occur.

If the campaigns and the moderators are successful at reducing the tensions to a level of comfortable conversation, the "debate" becomes too comfortable. Indeed, many focus groups reflect that few viewers remember anything said at a sitting debate. Instead, if anything, they remember something they saw.

Most voters cannot even remember ever seeing a sitting

debate. As a result, seated debates are typically nonevents with no winners and no losers. Of course, for the candidate who is a heavy favorite, this is great. If the candidate is an underdog seeking to close political ground, it is a lost opportunity.

But the risks of a seated event extend much further than becoming a nonevent. Relaxed candidates can be dangerous candidates. Seated debates can create candidates who are too relaxed. They slouch, twirl their chair, let their mind wander, or otherwise lose focus.

Like riding a motorcycle, seated debates are the most dangerous when the candidate feels the most comfortable and the least risk. It is just then that discipline of the debate preparation wears off, the details of the campaign strategy plan fade, and accidents happen.

In most elections, a significant part of every candidate's strategy is making the other candidate appear completely unacceptable—personally, professionally, and in every other way. Yet, in a seated debate where the candidates are seated at the same table, having a cordial conversation and displaying civility if not acceptability, this strategic goal is diluted, if not outright extinguished.

What is a voter to believe—what they hear about just how bad the opponent is or what the voter sees—two people seated together, casually discussing the issues in a cordial matter?

The seating arrangement offers little room for adaptation. The candidates are simply too close to confront each other aggressively; but absent differentiation resulting from candidates challenging each other, the debate may lose energy and meaning.

Given the physical proximity of all the participants, any attempt to escalate the tensions consistent with rejection can be risky. Should one candidate attempt to ratchet up the attacks on the other, either personally or professionally, it could be awkward at best.

If things got too heated, the physical proximity could lead to the possibility of the worst of all possibilities—an actual fight. One can lose hours on YouTube watching videos of politicians physically fighting each other—suffice it to say no one wins in these scenarios.

With that said, seated debates do offer some opportunities for unusual circumstances. For example, if an opponent has a nervous knee, is grossly overweight, avoids personal confrontation, or something similar, then a seated debate might make sense.

At a table, the knee will clearly bobble up and down. For the overweight, it will be difficult to comfortably fit in a chair (and, even if put on the end, will look unsightly). And for those opponents that are confrontation averse, close proximity can render them uncharacteristically silent or outright angry.

Podiums cover all of this up. The only part the audience sees is from the chest up. Meanwhile, the podium serves like a shield from which bombs and grenades can be launched. If candidates want to strip those away from an opponent while avoiding the challenges for themselves of where or how to stand, then the seated debate format might be the best choice.

The Townhall Debate

The latest trend in debates is commonly known as "townhall debates." Like a NASCAR race where the spectators are waiting on the seemingly inevitable collision, townhall debates engender the same kind of anticipation.

Townhall debates unleash the candidates from podiums

or seats to roam around the stage. They take away the shield of the podium and force the candidates into the arena where they must directly confront their opponents and voters.

Questions can come from the moderator, the audience (both those in attendance and those watching through social media), and the opponent. Lively exchanges can ensue, with time limitations thrown out the proverbial window. When not prevented by the number of candidates, it is the most preferred format for broadcast media, often yielding lots of action that can attract lots of viewers.

Moderators optimally manage the "political roller derby" to make sure that each candidate has an opportunity to speak on a topic and that both sides get approximately the same amount of time. Other than that, townhall debates can become the political debate version of "Open Mic Night," with lots of potential risk and reward.

The opportunities for miscues abound as the questions can come from any direction (including left field or the parking lot outside the stadium!) and raise any topic. Rather than manage the candidates, most moderators see their role akin to a hockey referee whose most important responsibility is to drop the puck to start the action.

In a townhall political debate, dropping the puck means throwing out a topic on which the moderator knows the candidates will jump decisively and fiercely. With the townhall style debate, neither candidate must be the villain, violating President Ronald Reagan's Eleventh Commandment against speaking ill of someone from the same political party.

Instead, the moderator eagerly assumes that role, creating an opening for the other candidate to seize the moment in a cloaked fashion. Effectively, candidates can say, "since it has been brought up, here is just how bad it is." The subject of the attack must then aggressively defend—not from the comfortable confines of a bordered podium but exposed on center stage with cameras running.

Of course, there is no reason that moderators cannot do the same in the other formats and often do. How to handle these situations substantively is discussed elsewhere. But, in the townhall format, they are the essence of the decision-making surrounding whether to agree to the format. That "red meat" Roman forum moment for political gladiators before the crowds must be considered carefully.

At the local level and even at the congressional level, townhall debates do not make sense. The requisite intensity simply does not exist at a level to support the kind of dynamics that makes such debates work for the candidates, the audience, or the media.

On the other hand, as interest rises and the campaign remains competitive and interesting, the chances are someone will suggest a townhall debate. Ultimately, the decision will again depend on the strengths and challenges of the candidates.

The most important consideration in deciding whether to agree to a townhall format is how can that format help enhance a candidate's chances of winning on Election Day. Since that day may come, every candidate should practice townhall meetings.

Other campaign books can detail both the advantages and disadvantages of townhall meetings as part of an election or re-election strategy. Regardless, if a townhall political debate is a possibility, then the candidate should have at least two or three townhall meetings beforehand. There is no substitute for having been in a townhall meeting in preparing for a townhall style political debate.

Two "never do this" exist for the townhall debate, one of which has already been discussed. First, do not invade the personal space of the other candidate. Voters do not like it and it never works out well. With a podium or seating, this rule is easily complied with (notwithstanding Senator Santorum's attempt). Just stay at your podium or in your seat.

With a townhall debate, it can be a little trickier. The simplest rule of thumb is for the candidate to stay "in your corner" or on the candidate's stool until it is the candidate's turn to speak. When that time comes, either move to the center of the stage or in the direction of the questioner or moderator. Never approach the political opponent. It just does not work out well.

And candidates should never turn their back to the questioner or the moderator when the candidate is being spoken to. In that regard, treat the moderator and the questioner as royalty.

Second, never make any sudden body movements. Calm and reassuring are the watchwords for a townhall debate, no matter how hot the room gets. The ability to demonstrate composure no matter what the circumstances is invaluable.

Sudden gestures, dramatic facial expressions, wild arm movements, sudden brisk walking, etc., all signal something other than calm resolve. Remember, voters want calm leaders, not frantic soldiers.

Similarly, pacing can be distracting, and candidates should avoid it. Townhall debates are all about body language—calm and measured. From there, the answers should do the rest of the work.

Well-done townhall debates are the most effective at connecting with a live audience. Bill Clinton's performance in the 1992 townhall debates is a good example of this (while then President George H.W. Bush's performance in the same debate is not). Because of this potential, in local elections with big audiences, the townhall format will give a candidate a unique opportunity to drive up enthusiasm among supporters and win over those sitting on the fence.

Unfortunately, townhall debates do not translate in the print media and are rarely captured in the broadcast media. What good vibrations may be occurring in the room between the candidate and the live audience rarely translates through the mediated filter of television or post-hoc newspaper reports.

If reaching voters not present at the debate is the primary factor in the decision-making process, then the risks of a townhall format more often than not will outweigh the advantages.

Multi-Candidate Debates

In recent years, the number of candidates challenging for their parties' nomination have literally skyrocketed. The myriad of reasons for the sudden increase in candidates is not as important as its reality in the new political world.

In 2016, Republicans had so many candidates for the GOP presidential nomination that they could not all fit on the same stage in GOP primary debates. For 2020, the Democratic field was, initially, even larger with numbers that necessitated multi-night debates among twenty candidates.

The question is how a candidate emerges from the pack as opposed to getting lost in the shuffle when the sheer number of candidates on the stage and the shortage of airtime make breaking out so difficult. Although the number of candidates decreases the opportunities to shine, it dramatically increases the need for preparation and separation, so when those fewer moments to shine do occur, the candidate is ready to make the most of them.

The impact of a full debate stage (or stages) is completely counterintuitive, since the average candidate would think less time, less preparation. The opposite is true. With so little time, the need to make the maximum impact with the least amount of time is huge.

In a quote about the relationship of preparation and time for speeches that has been attributed to a variety of public figures, the logic is explained thusly:

"It depends. If I am to speak ten minutes, I need a week for preparation; if fifteen minutes, three days; if half an hour, two days; if an hour, I am ready now." Regardless of the originator, it is sage advice that holds true for political debates.

If there was one thing that the 2016 presidential election proved, it was that media pundits and personalities have no greater insight into which candidates will win than anyone else. None of them thought that businessman Donald Trump would win the GOP nomination, much less defeat the Democratic presidential nominee Hillary Clinton.

In fact, throughout the 2016 presidential primaries and election, pundits and pollsters repeatedly pronounced dead-on-arrival as far as political professionals were concerned. But they were wrong—repeatedly wrong. No candidate should let them decide whether they get to be on the stage and, if on the stage, where they get to stand.

The same miscalculations happened in 2020. Many pundits declared Vice President Joe Biden as the "walking dead." Yet, he emerged from the long pre-nomination and nomination process as the Democratic nominee. That these two examples offer candidates who strike very different tones only reinforces the point.

In this environment, beware of media-sponsored debates. They are focused on one thing: ratings. The media wants viewers, but that is not all bad. Candidates want viewers too. The important distinction is how each want to attract viewers to political debates.

As cable news has proven, most media outlets, especially those focused on political coverage, prefer debates resembling the Coliseum games of Ancient Rome. For pundits and political promoters, it is political blood sport that sells.

While such formats may be good for attracting viewers, it is not so good for the participants, especially for those with one last political fight in the general election. Indeed, such a process often leaves the eventual winners so scarred and marred that their chances in the general election suffer seriously.

Certainly, a healthy dose of controversy between the candidates on the stage will increase the chances of big Nielsen ratings and improve the chances that a candidate emerges from the pack. On the other hand, taken to the extreme, it can easily result in the candidate winning the battle while losing the war.

The appropriate mix of public service, name recognition, fundraising war chest, polling data, ground game with political infrastructure, and other indicia of the ability to win is a tough one. Inevitably, it will be the product of some serious negotiations among the debate sponsor, the campaigns, the political parties, and the candidates.

Fortunately, being at the center of the stage is not the end all. As a result, it is probably not worth the money or effort to change locations on the debate stage for a single debate. But to not make the stage at all would be an enormous blow to any campaign, as born out in 2016 and 2020. More significantly, the incremental cost of recovering from missing the stage is just too great to not make every effort to stay on the main stage.

For anyone who has watched a crowded debate stage, the advantages and disadvantages of stage positioning are rather obvious. Most debate sponsors put the "frontrunner" at the center of the stage and the perceived least viable candidates on the ends. Voters know this and the body language of the candidates themselves confirm it.

Candidates stuck on the ends inevitably struggle to get time and exposure and often get left out of the debate entirely. Optically, they appear awkward, constantly having to turn toward the others, like the child stuck inside while the other kids in the neighborhood are playing outside. On the other hand, the candidate in the middle can feel like a piñata, the constant target from attacks on all sides.

Make no mistake, a candidate's strategy in the debate is directly impacted by the candidate's spot on the stage. Frontrunners standing in the middle of the stage must be prepared to handle attacks from multiple fronts. Marginal candidates at the ends must find ways to shift the center of gravity in their direction on issues that make them relevant to the debate.

With that dynamic in mind, many believe the optimal positioning is not in the middle and not on the end. Beyond that, the "win" in working the system in a multi-candidate debate is to make the stage to left or right of center.

Remember, candidates who talk the most about the issues they want to talk about win. The question is how to make that happen given the dynamics of the debate stage. In the 2016

GOP presidential debates, President Trump successfully made the debates about him. The result was that each successive debate increasingly focused on him.

Even in the debate that President Trump skipped entirely, he was nonetheless the center of attention. Of course, not every candidate has the experience of starring in their reality TV show and trying to emulate the unique personality traits of someone with a very different skill set is likely to end badly.

In multi-candidate primaries or elections, it is important to think of the political debates as a process as opposed to a series of isolated political events. In the earliest phases of the debates, the focus is inevitably commanding a plurality of support as opposed to a majority. The techniques for producing an early plurality capable of growing into an outright majority are very different than just focusing on winning over a majority of voters from day one.

The evolution of plurality to majority is one of building voter loyalty by separation on a series of issues. Successful candidates separate themselves from the rest of the pack by succinct positions that are important to constituencies that place one issue or set of issues above all other issues.

Early debates offer that opportunity to be different—authentically different—on priorities that distinguish the candidate from the rest. President Trump's divergence from the free trade orthodoxy that had dominated Republican policy advocacy for decades is an example of this, allowing him to condemn NAFTA in ways that Senators McCain and Romney were unable to do as Republican presidential candidates.

Multi-candidate primary debates are thus a building process—one brick at a time. A political debate in which voters cannot distinguish any one candidate from the rest is a lost opportunity. As a result, candidates must look for those opportunities to stand alone, assuming the risks of being out of line with the rest, to separate themselves from the rest.

Probably the best example was President Trump's willingness to be the only candidate to say that he would not commit to support the GOP nominee regardless of who it is. For every voter that wanted something new, someone new, President Trump earned their consideration with that simple gesture.

It was not a policy stance, nor even a promise that could be effectively enforced (how much weight does the support of a losing primary candidate really matter?), but it had symbolic weight.

President Trump separated himself from the pack and created a dynamic where it was the pack or him. At that moment, he had earned a spot in the finals. It was a high stakes decision. But, to make the finals, high stakes decisions are a necessary part (especially for an "outsider" candidate with little, if any, prior connection to the party).

Separation does not mean isolation. If candidates move so far out of the mainstream of what the loyal voters of the party to whom they are touting their candidacy, they will inevitably face the risk of irrelevancy. It is one thing to be different. It is quite another to lack credibility because the candidate's views or plans are so far out there that no one takes them seriously.

Merit alone is not the measure for determining whether a candidate's views have gotten too far out of the mainstream. In the 2012 Florida presidential primary, former Speaker Newt Gingrich proposed and defended the idea of putting a colony on the moon. With the help of the mainstream media, Senator Mitt Romney seized on it.

So much time had passed since man's landing on the moon.

The suggestion appeared disconnected to, or even dismissive of, the interests of contemporary voters. Senator Romney went so far as to suggest that if a CEO came to him with that kind of idea, he would fire him.

With thought, Speaker Gingrich's comeback would have been an easy retort: "Would Senator Romney have fired President John F. Kennedy when he suggested putting a man on the moon decades earlier?" But no such retort occurred, and Senator Romney and the media had a field day.

There are many legitimate reasons for national governments to consider space colonization, but political debates are rarely the time and place for such bold plans. That single answer did not cost Speaker Gingrich the GOP nomination, but it did create enough doubt to make the distance between Speaker Gingrich and the GOP nomination too far.

Early on, the 2020 Democratic nomination for president started to show signs of candidates getting "too far out there" for their own consultants. In primaries, the natural tendencies are to move to the extremes to secure some base or group of devoted followers, regardless of anything else.

And in a field of so many candidates, the temptation to "stick out and be different" can lure a candidate into going too far. Taken to the extreme, it prompts candidates to offer plans that have no basis and call into question the candidate's judgement and viability. It is one of the "bipartisan" dangers of political debates.

Within this context, the goal in a multi-candidate primary debate is to avoid the margins. Do not be the candidate that sounds like everyone else on the stage. On the other hand, do not be the candidate that is the most extreme on any serious issue.

By leaving some room for maneuvering, candidates can

adjust as the primary process progresses. It is possible to own the extreme and win. It is just not the preferred starting point. Let other candidates test the extreme and then move accordingly.

With one exception, the strategy of avoiding extremes applies across the board in a multi-candidate primary debate. In application, this means that no candidate should be the loudest, angriest, funniest, most boring, or any other extreme in presentation. Candidates who do not avoid the extremes win the prize for being the loudest, angriest, funniest, etc. but rarely win the election.

One exception does exist: candidates perceived to be authentic almost always do well. Once voters can be persuaded to turn off their inherent filters against accepting at face value what any politician says, the candidate's message can get through. For President Trump, like him or hate him, voters believed him.

By being willing to say what other politicians would deem too outrageous or unconventional, he convinced many voters that they could believe that he said what he meant and meant what he said. At that moment, he emerged as the candidate to beat.

This approach is much easier for challengers than incumbents, who are stuck defending their record, which nearly always aligns with middle-of-the-road politics.

Importantly, multi-candidate debates are not exceptions to the first rule of winning political debates: ***the candidates who talk about the things they want to talk about the most win.***

To the extent that a candidate or campaign has any input regarding how many candidates to let into the debate, there are a few things to consider. The number of candidates allowed to participate in a political debate impacts every other aspect of the debate, including some of the most important things, such as how long and how many opportunities each candidate gets to speak.

Undoubtedly, every debate will allow each candidate to speak at least once; otherwise, there is no reason to be there. With this starting point, candidates or their teams can determine the optimal number of candidates given the allocated time for the debate.

Obviously, campaigns should push for a number of candidates to be included so their candidate is on stage. From there, try to determine what is the optimal number to give the candidate the chance to shine against weaker opponents while also still giving them enough time to deliver their message. It does involve math.

For example, assuming a typical ninety-minute debate of six candidates translates into approximately ten minutes of speaking time, with all other things (the preliminary instructions, openings, and closings) taking the rest of the time.

If the number of candidates increases to ten, the amount of time that each candidate typically gets then drops to just over five minutes. These kinds of calculations illustrate why the number of candidates is so important.

Never lose sight of what is most important—getting on the debate stage. If a candidate is ranked eighth among candidates in the criteria for candidate participation and placement, then getting the number of candidates down to seven is self-defeating.

Getting fewer minutes because there are more candidates is far better than getting zero minutes because the candidate does not make the stage at all. In the beginning, the tendency (as illustrated by the 2016 GOP presidential primary or the 2020 Democratic presidential primary) is for more candidates early in the process to assure most credible candidates at least get a shot.

Over the course of the election, the opposite will start to happen. Some of that will be based on the inability of weaker candidates to produce; some of it will be the political parties asserting greater control of the direction of the election contest; and some of it will be sponsors attempting to make the debates more meaningful, with fewer candidates and more participation.

In addition to the number of candidates, there will be other things that can be decided before the debates begin. For example, multi-candidate debates are a good example of where the candidates can benefit by agreeing on what everyone calls each other on stage.

Candidates with impressive titles such as governors, senators, and other incumbents should prefer to be called by their title. Debates where all the candidates have similar rank may decide to drop the titles and make it a much more personal affair.

One of the toughest issues in multi-candidate debates is rebuttal time. If there are lots of candidates, it is impossible to allow every candidate to have rebuttal time.

On the other hand, it is not really fair to limit rebuttals to just one person or, worse yet, let the moderator or the candidates decide. The recent trend of automatically allowing a rebuttal by the candidate who was mentioned by name is evidence of how shallow these determinations can be.

Decide what the criteria is to get a rebuttal and then integrate it into the debate strategy. For example, if the rule is that any candidate whose name is said gets a rebuttal, then be careful in using other candidate's names.

No single issue is subject to more abuse during multi-candidate debates than the right to rebuttals, the time limitations that apply, and when to cut them off.

Some campaigns opt for no rebuttals. After all, it does typically involve giving moderators discretion, which is always risky business. Other candidates and campaigns opt for one rebuttal or objectively enforceable guidelines to assure that all candidates are treated equally. Unfortunately, such arbitrary enforceable rules that do not in some way take into consideration the flow of the debate can create awkward moments in a debate.

Of course, there is a third option which has become routine for many candidates in the modern political world—just ignore all the rules. While there does have to be some pretense for speaking out of turn, it rarely requires much. Simple righteous indignation is typically enough.

After all, defending one's honor is usually enough to get by with one or two infractions of the rules on rebuttals and time limitations. And even then, it typically draws no more than a warning. Disqualification is not a realistic consequence.

It is possible to request more time during a political debate. It is not unusual for a candidate to raise a hand, give a nod, or just start to speak. How the moderator or the audience will react is anyone's guess. As a result, a debate participant should carefully weigh the benefit of what might be gained versus the response for a rule violation.

Little good comes from attempting to assume the role of the timekeeper or enforcer. In most situations, the candidate comes across as the whiny child in the first row in third grade snitching on the other students. Based on attempts in the past, there is just no good way to do it.

That is not to say that no candidate has called time on another candidate who has gone over the agreed time restriction. It is often done. It just never produces good results. The candidate that speaks too long is unlikely to stop. And the reporting candidate's reputation evolves from viable candidate to tattletale. It is just not worth it, absent serious abuse.

One other good rule in a multi-candidate debate is stay at the podium. If the 2016 GOP presidential debates proved anything, they proved that aberrational body movements produce negative reactions by viewers and voters.

For example, drifting from the podium, staring aimlessly in the sky, waving at a member of the audience, and leaning heavily on the podium suggest a candidate that has lost interest. Stay engaged and use the podium to act the part of an interested candidate. When note-taking is allowed, appearing to do so signals attentiveness and engagement.

If a candidate cannot remain focused on a political debate for an office they feel is important, voters have reason to doubt whether the candidate can remain focused in office when confronted with endless strings of speeches, attacks, and potential boredom. The debate affords the opportunity to prove that a candidate can stay focused and engaged.

Because the media loves controversy, one common format suggestion in multi-party debates (and sometimes in just two-party debates) is candidate-to-candidate questioning. Basically, the idea is that candidates (and their campaign teams) have the most dirt and/or negative information against their opponents. Who better to pose questions positioned to leverage the most damaging information about a candidate than their opponents?

Should this procedure be agreed, two different objectives must be kept in mind to fully prepare a candidate: which questions to be ready to ask and which questions to be ready to answer. The techniques and strategies associated with these two debate dynamics are very different and involve completely different objectives, tactics, and preparations.

Like offense and defense in sports, both are necessary for success, yet distinct in what they entail. While common elements may seem apparent, they are indeed illusions.

When on the attack, remember the very act of questioning another candidate is adversarial by its nature, regardless of the intent of the questioner. Sometimes candidates believe that they can score "nice" points by asking largely meaningless questions to avoid the appearance of meanness or vitriol. Do not think that.

Such a tactic is a complete waste of one of the most valuable commodities that a candidate has in a debate—time. Essentially, the candidate is ceding time to the opponent to avoid appearing meanspirited. This is not a good reason to give away such a valuable commodity.

On the other hand, vitriolic or personal attacks are also never the answer. Well-trained debaters shrug off vitriolic attacks as irrational madness confirming that the candidate has neither the temperament nor judgment to serve. The voting audience frequently has the same reaction.

Success is not in the middle. Instead, when posing questions, candidates must be on offense with a clear understanding that the real goal is to score a point by forcing the conversation (debate) to topics the opponent does not want to talk about.

Winning the debate is talking about the things the candidate wants to talk about while keeping the opponent from talking about what they want to talk about. Questions that move the center of the debate in that direction are worth the effort.

And even better, they are things that can be prepared in advance of the debate based on research the campaign has done. So, there should be fewer surprises. Although a Perry Mason moment (a question so devastating that the opponent cannot recover) is possible, it almost never happens.

Instead, victory comes from a series of scored points, steadily building a lead that becomes insurmountable. This insurmountable lead is like a portrait of their opponent that the opponent cannot shake.

With this strategy in mind, the starting point is to identify what the candidate wants voters to associate with their opponent. Typically, it begins with pushing an opponent from ambiguity on tough issues to certainty that they now must defend.

Thus, the best opening questions are simple, clear, and straightforward, using the opponent's own words and positions to lock them into those positions for all the campaign to come. The goal is to create a mile marker toward a destination that the candidate need never spend time on again.

Campaigns benefit most from their opponent's own voice providing the line of attack. "I voted for the war before I voted against it"—the most memorable words from Democratic presidential nominee John Kerry and a deathblow to his candidacy.

Because these were his own words, it was next to impossible for Senator Kerry to deny them; he could only try to explain them. Every moment that candidates spend explaining, they are losing the most important commodity they have—time to talk about what they want to talk about.

Because there are no rules dictating what a candidate can or cannot say, the debate format does not have to explicitly permit candidate questioning for candidates to ask questions. Any candidate can ask any other candidate a question at any time regardless of the format. Admittedly, opponents do not have to answer (even if the rules contemplate candidate questioning).

Yet, piercing questions demanding an answer do exactly that—demand an answer. Candidates can only rarely get away with simply responding by saying "The debate rules do not require me to answer and so I am not going to answer that question."

But that is only true for questions that inherently demand an answer to the question. For other questions, especially rhetorical ones, the opposing candidate can simply ignore the question and follow the first rule of debates—talk about the things the candidate wants to talk about.

The best questions can also be those to which there is no good answer. More often than not, they are questions that seek the confirmation of an objectively provable fact. This necessarily excludes questions seeking an explanation or an opinion. If the question begins with the word "why," it is undoubtedly a bad question, only giving an opponent time to justify or explain away an embarrassing fact.

A statement of an embarrassing fact followed by "isn't that true?" is not really a question to be answered directly yet can be very effective. As a threshold, it can force the opposing candidate to confirm in their own voice the embarrassing fact. But it can do more.

Sometimes, candidates need to prove a "negative"—something that did not happen. Or the candidate wants to prove that the opposing candidate has not and will not do something:

"The fact is that you have never voted for a tax cut, isn't that true?"

"You have voted for every single proposed tax increase that came before you, isn't that true?"

"You have more DUI convictions than all the other candidates in this race combined, isn't that true?"

In these circumstances, let the questions do the work. The answers (or lack thereof) will do the rest. The challenge is to craft the right question for the right moment.

Then, keep asking the question until the opposing candidate delivers an acceptable response. If the opposing candidate does not, keep asking it. There is no reason to stop doing that which works.

For multi-candidate debates, (and even two-person debates), make them memorable. Ask ten people to describe the last political debate that they watched and see what happens. Do not be surprised if they cannot, or, if they vaguely describe one, it was a debate where something memorable happened. And, oddly enough, the memorable moment rarely involves any issue heavily contested in the election involved.

As evidenced by the eagerness of networks to televise debates and the Nielsen ratings to support them, people *do watch* debates. Absent some serious gaffe, emotional breakdown, or completely unexpected event, no one remembers them. In fact, most candidates do not even remember them.

For heavily favored incumbents, a forgotten debate is a good thing. For a candidate struggling to break out of a crowded field, it is a horrible thing.

So, what are the options for moving the "memorability" needle? First, figure out what kind of memory works best for winning the election. Memorability alone should never be the objective.

For example, candidates who just want to be remembered could always show up for the debate in a clown outfit. Everyone would likely remember the candidate. No one would vote for them. The best opportunities involve one of two possibilities: unshakable facts and the element of surprise. Combine the two and a candidate can create that magic moment that no one expected.

Spontaneity is rarely good for the unprepared candidate forced to respond to something no one has discussed. The truth can be devastating when unexpected and with a sharp edge. It is why opposition research is so valuable. The best preparation focuses on creating the dynamics for just such a "surprise" moment.

Of course, as President Reagan proved, humor can be just as effective since most people remember a good laugh. But candidates are not natural comedians. Instead, as President Reagan proved, the best one-liners are those practiced, tweaked, tested, and delivered smoothly and effortlessly.

Making it memorable can be as simple as just giving voters something they can remember and repeat. So, it has to be more than just more talk; it has to leave an impression.

CHAPTER 10

OPENINGS & CLOSINGS

Two parts of political debates that have not varied much in different formats are openings and closings. Of course, this does presuppose there are openings and closings. Increasingly in modern political debates, openings and closings are being considered optional. This is largely the product of media outlets wanting to "cut to the chase" since they regard time spent on openings and closings as wasted.

Certainly, as an election season progresses, the need for openings and closings may diminish as viewers and voters become increasingly familiar with who the candidates are. Yet, until that level of familiarity does exist, such as at the beginning of the election season or if there are only a handful of debates, openings serve a very important role, namely introducing the candidates.

Openings, aptly named, begin the debate by offering candidates a chance to introduce themselves, telling voters who they are, what they stand for, and what they want. No one should underestimate the importance of this moment and opportunity.

In most debates, openings are preceded by some preliminary remarks from the sponsor of the debate or the moderator. In addition, the moderator may highlight some of the ground rules for the debate, including limitations (if any) on audience reaction.

Generally, it is a good practice for the sponsor or moderator of the debate to identify everyone in the "production" of the debate, including the timekeeper, floor managers, and others associated with the actual production of the debate. This allows everyone to know the identity of everyone else, creating the necessary transparency to serve as an effective check to make sure everyone is doing their job in an impartial and fair way.

Subject only to those preliminary remarks about others, openings are the first opportunity in a political debate for candidates to address voters in an unfiltered way. While the campaigns and others may have spent lots of money defining the candidates, the real first impressions of candidates often really begin with the candidates' first opening in the first debate.

Given the television ratings for presidential debates, compared to other campaign events, it is likely that millions of voters will be witnessing for the first time the candidates speak for a substantial length of time, uninterrupted. In the real world, there are no second "first impressions." So, this is a critically important moment—a candidate constructing voters' first impression of who the candidate is.

When that moment comes, optimally all the rules will have been negotiated and agreed to, the moderator identified and vetted, and mechanisms established to police the debate for fairness and balance. Think of this moment in these terms: lights, camera, action: the opening.

There is no good excuse for a candidate to not have a good opening. After all, everyone knows well in advance of the debate the who, what, when, and where for this critically important moment. At that time and place, the candidate has the most control that they will have during the entire election contest.

The candidates literally and figuratively can say whatever they want—about themselves, their opponents, the issues, and election. Voters can see the candidates, their faces, expressions, and mannerisms. Voters can hear the candidates—their voice, tone, and content. No candidate will ever have more control over what the candidate wants voters to know than in the opening and, subsequently, in the closing.

For a candidate's supporters and opponents, the opening will not change much of anything, including any minds. After the opening, and then the closing (absent a real gaffe), supporters will still support the candidate, and opponents will still oppose the candidate.

On the other hand, for the few undecided voters (who may have never seen either of the candidates before), it will be the first (and sometimes only) opportunity to see the candidates for themselves. Underscoring the point, studies show that over half of jurors in a jury trial setting (much like voters in the political world) make up their minds after opening statements.

After openings, most decision makers, whether voters or jurors, move into a time of "tending" their mental choice. This includes rationalizing away negative information, identifying reinforcing information, and otherwise tending the mental image they have of the candidate.

The only real variable with openings is which candidate goes first. In the scheme of things, it really makes little difference. With very few exceptions, no one watching a debate typically even remembers which candidate went first and which candidate went last.

When someone does remember, it makes no difference. Since there is no "burden of proof" as exists in a jury trial, the sequence of speakers really makes no difference.

Perhaps there is some advantage to going first, since a candidate can attempt to set the tone or dictate the opening issues. But whoever goes second gets a chance to respond early to that which has been injected into the debate. While some may differ, the truth is that sequencing between first and second is largely a distinction without a difference.

No opening should last less than one minute nor more than three minutes. One minute is the least amount of time for candidates to meaningfully introduce themselves and to provide some outline of the issues. Anything over three minutes is a waste of time, since the average person starts to tune out after roughly three minutes of continuous talking.

The importance of the moment does not extend the attention span of the average person—even at the beginning of an important political debate. Consider interpersonal conversations. Conversation does not technically begin until more than one person communicates, and if one person goes on and on right off the bat, no conversation will be developed.

Generally, no one should start with an opening that lasts longer than about three minutes. At that moment, minds begin to wander.

Openings should be between 90 and 180 seconds. A little more than two-minutes is optimal: enough time for an introduction, a summary of the issues, and a specific request that viewers cast their ballots for the candidate. The debate will offer plenty of time for the details of plans and positions. It is a mistake to try to say everything in the opening—either by talking too quickly or going way overtime.

Some candidates prefer to write down their opening and

then memorize it or use notecards or a teleprompter. Other candidates prefer to deliver their opening extemporaneously, using bullet points as reminders or rehearsed language patterns.

There are numerous examples where each technique has worked. There is no universal approach that will work for every candidate. Like the different formats, the strengths and weaknesses of the candidates should guide which method is employed.

A successful debate advances the objective of the campaign strategy to win the Election Day. As a result, the most consistently reliable technique for developing an opening is a collective, collaborative draft written and edited by the entire campaign team, considering all the strategies and challenges on the table.

Once a draft has been completed, the candidate should carefully review and, if appropriate, edit the draft opening to put the speech in the candidate's voice. If it does not sound like something the candidate would say or how the candidate would say it, it will not convey authenticity and voters will notice.

Let the entire team look at the revised draft opening. The goal is to get it right, and the more eyes and minds looking at the opening only increase the chances of getting it right. No good reasons exist to take unnecessary risks on untested content or marginally acceptable phrases.

Every word should be vetted for reaction and effectiveness. In a debate, there are lots of questions and answers. But there is only one opening and, hence, there is a very high premium on getting it exactly right.

Accuracy is essential. Never give a political opponent an easy "gimme" with a simple mistake easily identified and quickly corrected. The failure to do so allows the political opponent to completely de-credential the candidate's entire opening by focusing solely on the one mistake made.

Humor is tempting but rarely works out well. And subtlety has no place in an opening or closing statement. The best rule is simple and straightforward: "mean what you say and say what you mean."

The beauty of getting the opening right is that a candidate can use it over and over again—rally after rally, event after event, and answer after answer. With so much focus on getting it right, it is also important to avoid letting perfect become the enemy of good.

There are good openings. There are no perfect openings. There will always be the one thing that a candidate or the campaign would do differently if they had the chance to do it again.

Moving closer and closer to perfection involves one simple concept: practice makes perfect. It is why candidates become better and better as the election campaign goes on. As the repetitions go up, the ease of delivery does, too.

It is just two minutes. Managing the two minutes may require hours, but it will be among the most important two minutes in the campaign. It is the one part of the debate that a candidate can most prepare.

Some might suggest, especially in contests with lots of debates, that the candidates skip the openings altogether. Typically, one campaign or the other will insist that the candidates and their positions on key issues are well-known, so why make them say it again. Of course, that presupposes that everyone at a subsequent debate attended an earlier debate. If the campaigns are doing their job, that is not true.

But, even if it was true, it does not change the need to say it again through an opening defining the candidate and what they are about. Even when candidates give the same opening, viewers hear something different every time they hear it.

Two possibilities exist for a strong opening. First, especially for new candidates focused on driving up name recognition, the candidate can begin with: "Hello! My name is Jane Doe, and I want to be your next State District 73 House member."

Second, the other option is to take advantage of the two most underutilized, but incredibly effective words in the English language: "Thank you!" For many candidates, the most difficult part of the debate is the first thirty seconds of the debate. Out of the box, they stutter and stop and search for words.

With the "thank you" beginning, the start becomes much more manageable. The candidate can thank the sponsors of the debate. Then thank the moderators, the questioners, and the opposing candidate. Thank supporters for attending.

And finally, thank voters for the opportunity to explain why they should vote for and support the candidate. By then, the candidate is into the flow of the debate.

The importance of this beginning cannot be overstated. It accomplishes two important purposes. First, everyone likes to hear "thank you." Beginning with thank you is a clear signal of respect and humility. Nothing bad happens from starting with it.

In addition, it is an easy way to start strongly and move on past the early debate jitters. By beginning with something as simple and innocuous as thank you, candidates can get started with little to no risk. From there, they can turn to the topics they need and want to talk about.

After "hello" or "thank you," with few exceptions, openings should raise the following topics:

- who the candidate is;
- what the candidate stands for; and,
- what the candidate wants—the viewer's vote.

With just a minute or two, time does not permit a full life story and most voters would not want to hear it all at once anyway.

Instead, crisp, succinct, and to-the-point statements paint a quick portrait of the candidate's life. There will be plenty of time to use life stories to explain a position or a point. For the opening, it should be a snapshot of who the candidate is.

After the "who," the opening should turn to a staccato series of the important issues in the election contest and where the candidate stands on them. No fewer than three nor more than five key issues, promises, platforms, or commitments will do.

Contrary to popular perception, the last part of an opening is as important as the other parts. Voters expect candidates to ask them for their vote. Most would think that such a request is a basic underlying assumption of qualifying and campaigning for public office. But it is not. Candidates should ask voters for their votes.

One place to ask is in the opening. Another place to ask is the closing. Candidates can never ask enough. Here is the most common ask: "And so, I humbly ask you to cast your ballot and to ask your friends and family to cast their ballot for me in this election."

Like openings, begin the closings with a simple "thank you." It provides the candidate with the opportunity to reorient from the rough and tumble of the debate into a more positive frame of mind. It also allows the candidate to summarize the positive points from the debate.

Finally, it can temper the flare-ups with the questioners and the moderator. "Thank you" are wonderful words and using them to end the debate can only lead to good things.

After "thank you," each candidate can make a final statement to the voters. This statement can be rehearsed from prepared scripts much like the opening statement or it can consist of a summary of what has happened at the debate.

For talented candidates, it is the opportunity to put a period (or even an exclamation point) on issues important to the campaign. Undertaking such an effort should be left to those who have proven their ability to deliver in such circumstances. Attempting it without the requisite skill set is a recipe for disaster.

Close with the same plea that started the debate: "And so, I humbly ask you to cast your ballot and to ask your friends and family to cast their ballot for me in this election." When delivering this line, look directly into the camera if the debate is televised. If not, look directly into the eyes of the audience. It is a moment—do not do anything to distract from it.

CHAPTER 11

ANSWERING THE QUESTIONS

As soon as the openings are over, someone, either the moderator or a panelist, will ask a question. Always listen to the question carefully.

There are three basic requirements for responding with a good answer: (1) never interrupt the questioner, attempting to answer before the question has been completed; (2) never attempt to answer a tougher question than was asked; (3) always provide answers that are consistent with the foundational message of the campaign.

Let the questioner finish the question. There is no good reason to rush the debate or the answer. The debate will not get any shorter just because a candidate cut off the question or rushed to answer. If it is a one-hour debate, then it will be a one-hour debate, regardless of how many answers get crunched into the allotted time.

Pause briefly—one thousand one; one thousand two; one thousand three. The most effective attorneys in the courtroom are the ones that control the rhythm of the discourse as opposed to becoming the victim of it. Forcing the pause puts the candidate in control of not only the rhythm of the debate but also the rhythm of the candidate. Maintaining self-control is one of the most important skill sets for controlling the debate.

Speak confidently. The pause should allow the candidate

to modulate what comes out when the candidate speaks. This is true for volume, pace, and tone. Practicing speaking confidently helps the most in learning to reliably speak confidently.

Sometimes, the questioner is asking a lot less than the candidate expects. There is no good reason to answer tough questions that were never asked.

Candidates do not earn "extra credit" for answering a tougher question than was asked. If asked to identify their stance on a tax issue, it does not help to provide more information than the basic answer requires. The candidate also risks including either incorrect information or details that can then be attacked.

Use all of the time allotted for the answer. Time communicating directly with voters is one of the most valuable commodities a candidate has.

If the rules permit two minutes for an answer, then the candidate should speak for the entire two minutes in answering the question. It may be that the candidate does not need the full two minutes to answer the question posed. This is not a good reason to use less than the full two minutes allotted.

Answer the question and then move on to one of the important themes of the candidate's campaign until the red light comes on, indicating that the candidate's time is up.

Do not look at, point at, or speak to the opponent. Remember, the point of the debate is not to persuade the opponent; maintain the focus where it should be, on the audience of voters.

Cross-stage stare contests, finger-pointing, and arguing with the opponent diminishes the candidate and give more airtime and focus for the opponent. Do not share the spotlight. Instead, own the time when it is the candidate's turn to speak.

Avoid excessive body movements. Waving arms, rolling eyes, head shaking, and hand gestures are distracting. It does not mean that a candidate must become stilted or stiff. It does mean that dramatic body movements while answering a question distract viewers from what the candidate is saying.

Avoid snorting, sighing, and groans. History is replete with examples of candidates doing all these things, much to the dismay of those watching the debate. Not only is it amateurish, but it reflects some level of a lack of self-control. No one will be persuaded by a candidate violently shaking the head no or sighing at an opponent's answer. Such conduct always hurts more than it helps.

Conceive of the answers to questions as an opportunity to have a conversation at the debate. Rather than a series of specific questions followed by well-framed answers, with each question and answer independent of the other, have a conversation.

This means thinking of the entirety of the debate as an opportunity to have a conversation with voters about a variety of topics, all of which involve who the candidate is, what the candidate thinks, where the candidate is from, and what the candidate will do.

Most debate formats not only include answers to questions but also give candidates the right to rebut an opponent's answer. Indeed, some formats include rebuttals to rebuttals, meaning there is a question, an answer, a rebuttal, and a final rebuttal.

Rebuttals are the opportunity for a candidate to directly attack an answer or response by their opponent. All of the rules for answers apply equally to rebuttals, including especially the rule that the candidate use all of the allocated time for rebuttal.

The most common mistake in rebuttals is an attempt by a candidate to attack every single item that an opponent says. More often than not, voters get lost in all of the points the candidate is attempting to make and the candidate gets lost in remembering all the things to attack.

The most effective rebuttals zero in on one or two items in the opponent's answer and respond to them. If the opponent is clearly wrong about something, point out the error in clear, concise, and decisive terms.

If it is a matter on which the candidates just differ, clearly articulate the difference in stark terms that anyone could understand. This might include something like, "My opponent believes that no crime is so bad as to warrant the death penalty; I, on the other hand, recognize that some crimes against humanity are so heinous that we as a society must respond with the ultimate penalty."

Sometimes, the opponent's answer includes nothing that the candidate believes merits a response. In other words, the opponent's answer did not damage. While the temptation might be to just let it go, do not waive the right to rebuttal. Instead, use the time to talk about the things important to the campaign until the time is up.

Remember, one of the most valuable commodities a candidate has is time to talk directly to the voters. The rebuttal time is exactly that—use it.

Finally, do not yield to invitations to get into a verbal slugfest. Certainly, moderators and panelists will try to tempt candidates into an onstage food fight, and desperate candidates will try everything to pull a candidate down into a street fight to create some level of parity between the candidates. Resist.

As the old warning about wrestling with a pig makes clear, you never win and only end up dirtying yourself. Composure, calm, confidence, and caring are all things that serve candidates well. More significantly, they leave lasting impressions that extend well beyond the end of the debate.

Of course, all of these suggestions reflect the "how" to answer. The content of the answers and rebuttals are dictated by many kinds of things. Most often they are dictated by the issues in the political campaign. Most often, the "what" of the debate is dictated by the respective campaign strategies of the campaigns of the candidates on the debate stage.

Communicating the "what" will be the most important part of the debate. A successful debate means a candidate's message lives on after the debate; that is the ultimate objective.

CHAPTER 12

ESSENTIAL TIPS FOR WINNING

Rule 1:
Candidates who talk the most about what they want to talk about win.

No one can *force* a candidate to talk about anything in a political debate. The key for candidates who want to win the debate is to talk more about what they want to talk about and as little as possible about what they do not. It requires discipline.

If the moderator asks about abortion when that is not what the candidate wants to focus on, the candidate should respond succinctly with no more than a few words (e.g., "As you know, I oppose it"). After providing a direct and brief response, candidates should then quickly pivot to spend the balance of their time discussing what they do want to talk about (e.g., economic policy, national security, etc.).

Think of it as the "Rule of the Color Red." What is your favorite food? Pizza, but let me explain the color Red. What is your favorite city? Phoenix, but let me tell you about the color Red. If the worst thing that happens is that candidates are accused of being non-responsive but have spent virtually the whole debate talking about the color Red, then they win.

Of course, the better debaters are the ones capable of coherently connecting what they want to discuss to the question they have been asked (tomato-based pizza sauce is red, the Phoenix landscape is reddish, etc.). Candidates should never take the bait from either the moderator or their opponents. To win, candidates should talk about Red, not the smears or attacks others want to use to distract and cause the candidate to struggle with an explanation.

Senator Bernie Sanders' relative success as a candidate can be explained in part by his message discipline ("relative" in the sense that he's a balding, self-identified Socialist and Independent, and somewhat curmudgeonly New Englander, yet managed to finish second in consecutive Democratic primary seasons). Some have complained that his debate performances sound an awful lot like his stump speeches.

That is no accident. His dedication to repeating what his campaign believes are tenets of his core message generates a *predictability* that translates into *authenticity*. What you see is what you get with Senator Sanders (unfortunately for him, that ceiling falls below the threshold of national electability).

Rule 2:
The real judges rarely remember words; they remember images.

Neither the media nor the pundits are the real judges of who wins a political debate; voters are. And, while they and the opponent will dissect every single word a candidate speaks, voters will remember very few of them (absent a total gaffe).

Instead, voters form images from what they see, hear, sense, and conclude. Working backward, candidates should decide what they want the audience to remember before they start and then stick to that image throughout the debate.

To stay on message, write what you want to be remembered

for at the top of your notepad the moment you walk up to the podium. Then, glance at it and formulate every response to fit and further that image. Be that image and voters will believe it is who you are. It should go without saying, but never pick an image you cannot be.

President Reagan's legendary line about not making age an issue in the 1984 campaign is an example of the power of this approach. He had not performed wonderfully in the debates that campaign season (including unforced errors with incorrect facts), yet none of that is remembered because he was able to deploy a tested line that reinforced his image as a witty, yet not mean-spirited, candidate who was like a wise grandparent. Yes, it was humorous, but the humor was consistent with, not contradictory of, the image he and his campaign team meticulously curated.

If done correctly, candidates can win the debate even if they are not the best debater. Winning the argument always beats winning the debate. Voters want someone they can believe, not necessarily someone who knows all the facts.

Rule 3:
Seek safe harbors whenever stormy seas arise.

No matter how prepared or talented a candidate is, uncomfortable moments can still occur during political debates. Sometimes it is a "gotcha" question; other times it is just a complete surprise. The key is for candidates to know their "safe harbors" when storms roll in.

"Safe harbors" are theme-based answers that work regardless of the question. Candidates should think about them and create them before the debate so they can be deployed smoothly when the need arises.

Most often, safe harbors involve elevating the conversation from the specific to the general. So, if the moderator asks about a specific piece of legislation (e.g., HB 1787) or a person (e.g., Jane Isolak) that the candidate does not know, they should never try to fake it. Instead they should explain their approach to legislation or their approach to dealing with other political or government leaders.

The key is to consider the question from the "next level up." For example, if the piece of legislation being asked about concerns energy and natural resources, the candidate should talk about their approach to energy policy.

Explaining the candidate's approach to decision-making is an excellent "catch-all" response when the details of the question being asked are a bit fuzzy. Candidates who explain they will "do my homework, listen to my constituents, consult experts in the area, apply my own values, and decide what is in the best interests of my country or state" have provided an answer that most voters will respect.

A candidate's ultimate safe harbor could be, "This is a good opportunity to actually explain to everyone my approach and what I will do regardless of the legislation or people involved. Here is my approach."

Most importantly, candidates should not let either the moderator or their opponents push them out of their safe harbor. So, if they push with "what about this specific bill or that particular person," candidates should be firmly resolved and exploit the opportunity—"I've answered that, but let me finish my thought about the color Red."

Rule 4:
Details never win debates, but mistakes can lose a debate.

Enormous pressure exists for candidates to spout off a series of numbers, percentages, and specifics. They should not give into the pressure. Anything less than perfection translates into an off-message story about how they got it wrong by some fact-checker looking to make a name off of candidates' mistakes.

"Crime is on the rise" works just as well as specifying that the number of murders in 2014 was 455, and the murders in 2017 was 478, and the murders in 2020 are already 480. If candidates go with specifics and get one number wrong, they lose the impact of their point *and* they also get pulled off message about the color Red.

If there are specific numbers, people, or places that candidates feel compelled to use, they should write them down on the pad the moment after they write the image they want to convey. Then, when the time is right, look down and recite them with accuracy and confidence.

Texas Governor Rick Perry's gaffe in a November 2011 Republican presidential primary debate stands out as the nightmare scenario. Having previously vowed to eliminate three executive agencies should he become president, the Governor was asked to identify which three he would cut. After quickly naming the first two, he froze, unable to recall (or even make up) the third.

There was no opportunity for a "do over." His candidacy, for all intents and purposes, was over. The lesson is clear: want to be specific? Be prepared to deliver. It is wiser to have more general points. No candidate has lost because of making generic claims about "bloated bureaucracy."

Rule 5:
Follow the rules, but no more than that.

Typically, the campaigns negotiate the format and rules of a debate before it starts. Other than those rules, candidates should not impose additional rules on themselves.

If an answer runs a little over the time limit or if candidates interject when they feel the need to, no one is going to disqualify them from the debate. On the other hand, candidates that routinely ignore the rules should not be surprised when voters react negatively. It is not worth the little extra that may be gained.

In addition, candidates should never follow nonexistent rules—for example, how they spend their time. No rule says a candidate must answer the question that was asked or that only moderators can ask questions. No rule says candidates must spend their entire two minutes on the topic the moderator asks about.

Also, no rule says a candidate cannot answer an opponent's question posed to them, even though it is not their turn. Remember, the more time spent talking about what the candidate wants to talk about, the more they are winning. Never yield back one minute of time or pass on an opportunity to talk about the color Red.

Finally, never accept implied rules based on assumed premises to which the candidate need not agree. As an illustration, if the airline were to ask customers, "Do you want to get there on time or safely?" the proper answer is "Both on time *and* safely."

Candidates can and should always refute what they believe are false premises. "Well, I don't accept the premise of your question, and here's why . . ." is a fine way to start a response.

Other implied assumptions can be a false statement of a candidate's record or past; similarly, these should never be accepted. If the assumption is incorrect, candidates should attack the question and correct the assumption; answering it as posed means falling into the questioner's trap.

Rule 6:
The moderator is never your friend.

Moderators are television personalities who want to be remembered; putting candidates in difficult positions is an easy way to do that. At no time in the debate should candidates assume the moderator/questioner are friends. They are not.

Two memorable examples of exchanges with moderators show how recognizing this (or failing to do so) can be the difference between winning and losing a debate. Regarding the latter scenario, Massachusetts Governor Michael Dukakis' response to a question from CNN's Bernard Shaw about the death penalty during the 1988 presidential debates is the epitome of "losing to the moderator/questioner."

Governor Dukakis was posed a hypothetical question about whether he would support the death penalty if his wife, Kitty, were raped and murdered. The graphic nature of the question itself, asking a candidate to theorize about the brutal treatment of their spouse, would be offensive to most people and certainly warrant an emotional, even justifiably angry, response.

Instead, Governor Dukakis' bland answer—a boilerplate mention of his lifelong opposition to capital punishment—

made *the candidate*, not the questioner, appear insensitive and uncaring. Want to articulate opposition to the death penalty? Do NOT do it this way.

Former House Speaker Gingrich's approach during the 2012 Republican presidential primary debates offers an excellent contrast. When CNN's John King started the debate by referencing a marital issue regarding the candidate's ex-wife and asking the candidate if he would like to respond, former Speaker Gingrich gave a lesson on how to deal with prickly moderators:

> *"No, but I will. I think the destructive, vicious, negative nature of much of the news media makes it harder to govern this country, harder to attract decent people to run for public office. And I am appalled that you would begin a presidential debate on a topic like that."*

The audience response was an immediate standing ovation. The Republican presidential primary debate in Charleston, South Carolina had just been won.

Even if your staff secured a loyal follower, the moderator is not your friend. In their zeal to help, they may end up being a hindrance. Regardless of the intent of the moderator, they should never be confused with the audience to whom you should be speaking; the voters are the audience.

Debates are not won by convincing the opponent, nor should the focus be convincing the moderator; always focus your responses on the people you are trying to persuade—the voters. Talking past the moderators, and directly to the voters, allows you to accomplish Rule 1: talk about the things you want to talk about.

Rule 7:
Nothing replaces a good genuine smile.

Research strongly confirms the communicative value of a smile. It takes enormous self-confidence, control, and discipline to smile regardless of the circumstances. The worse it gets, the more candidates smile—appear at ease and the world may smile with them. Lose that smile and risk losing the audience.

Obviously, for some topics, smiling is inappropriate. How would the audience react to a candidate obliviously smiling as a question is asked about a danger facing Americans? Disgust ("How can this candidate smile at a time like this?") and condemnation ("This candidate is not authentic, just faking a smile all the time") most likely.

Most answers can be provided (and boosted with) a smile because optimistic answers with solutions for a better future routinely beat scowls of intimidation and fear. Candidates want to be remembered as cheerful warriors, not angry pessimists.

Notably, smiling is not simply the display of teeth. It must be genuine. Most psychologists say the best smiles come from a "happy place." Most voters want leaders that have a "happy place" accessible to them as well. There is no substitute for confidently saying "follow me in the pursuit of happiness" with a genuine smile for every voter, whatever their circumstance.

Rule 8:
Debaters who think the least but say the most during the debate have the best chance to win.

Prepared competitors sometimes defeat more talented opponents who are less prepared, and yes, talented competitors sometimes defeat less talented but better-prepared opponents. But most importantly, better-prepared competitors *always* defeat equally talented opponents. In all cases, practice improves performance. In sports, repetition at increasing speeds of the same swing, jump shot, or pass play lead to optimal outcomes. Eventually, what is practiced becomes instinctive— precise and fast. Debating is no different; practicing responses leads to better answers with less effort and fewer missed opportunities.

MAKE NO MISTAKE; MEMORIZATION IS NOT EFFECTIVE PRACTICE. The ideal is to react instinctively to a verbal cue with a set of answers that include the topics the candidate wants to talk about. Except for the first sentence and the last sentence of a debate, memorization is never a good idea.

Repetitive, memorized lines can lead to disaster. That is what happened to Senator Marco Rubio in the 2016 Republican presidential primary debates when former Governor Chris Christie mocked him for his robotic-like repetition of the line that President Obama "knows exactly what he is doing."

That one moment reversed any momentum the Rubio campaign had and left him reeling. Emphasizing the core message does not require repeating the same rehearsed lines over and over again.

The best tool for practice is cue cards with one word on one side of a card and a list of topics on the other. As an example, the one-word trigger might be "women"; the topics might be (a) the opponent's record on women's issues, (b) the opponent's bad comments on women or women's issues, and (c) the candidate's great record on women's issues. The goal is to instinctively connect the two.

Of course, the one word should cover a whole category of questions. As your response becomes automatic, it leaves you with the confidence to follow Rule 1 but in the context of instinctive answers. Although the response may be a list, never number the items on the list. Numbering a list unnecessarily risks creating awkward moments when the candidate cannot remember all of the list. So, just start with "first" and then say "next."

Finally, as President Ronald Reagan proved in the first debate in 1984 (and Ed Rollins confirms), you can be over-prepared. When this happens, you have more information stuffed in your head than you can possibly use. For this reason, never use more than five to seven cue cards. Anything more than that is just asking for trouble.

Rule 9:
Anger is a debater's worst enemy and best friend.

Angry responses are just that—angry responses. The key is to recognize it and use it advantageously. Here are the key steps.

First, candidates must be able to control their temper. Those who struggle to do so must train themselves to self-diagnose when they are getting angry and know what to do in response. When candidates sense they are feeling anger, they should be conditioned to go to their core message (the color Red) or a safe harbor. Candidates should not try to talk their way out of it; it never ends well.

Second, candidates would do well to learn what makes their opponent angry and how to spot when they are angry. When that happens, it is an opportune moment. Angry people act irrationally, say stupid things they regret, and otherwise lose composure.

Finally, test candidates in practice debates, calling them a "liar" and other outlandish insults. A candidate's reaction cannot be predicted and addressed until it happens in live action. Then rehearse measured responses, transitioning to the color Red, or docking in safe harbors. Practice it before the debate, and the moment when the rest of the world is watching will not be the first time they had to defend against a hit below the belt.

This does not mean there is never a place for *controlled* anger in a debate. The example of former House Speaker Gingrich's takedown of John King shows how skilled candidates can use angry moments to their advantage. Two points reveal the strategic brilliance of his response.

First, after the initial applause had died down, former Speaker Gingrich asked to continue and directly addressed the substance of the question—refuting the veracity of the allegations and concluding with a unifying message for all the parties' candidates being attacked by "the elite media." This simultaneously upheld former President Reagan's 11th Commandment and played to the general public's skepticism of media (and received another standing ovation).

Just as importantly, the candidate's reflections after the debate revealed his complete understanding and control of the situation. When interviewed afterward by CNN's Anderson Cooper, former Speaker Gingrich gave King good marks: "I thought it was a terrific debate for all of us. The audience was appreciative. I thought John did a great job. It was direct; it was tough. You could see the differences."

Now perhaps "great" slightly inflated his evaluation of the moderator, but the veteran Congressman understood the moment (he had clearly won the night) and knew better than to diminish the positive spotlight being shown on him by refocusing it negatively on the moderator.

The former Speaker is also a veteran of debate, and he knew very well that King's question teed him up for a game-changing moment. Political debates are not tea parties—they can get (some argue, *should*) get heated. Candidates who can maintain a level head will be better positioned to recognize strategic opportunities and capitalize on them.

Rule 10:
Mental boredom allows your opponent to control the debate.

The moment President George H. W. Bush looked at his watch in the 1992 presidential townhall debate, he did more than appear disinterested in a debate about the future of the country; he lost control. From that moment forward, President Clinton controlled the flow of the debate.

Like sporting events, mistakes near the end of debates can be magnified. This is also when candidates are most likely to become bored, losing touch with the moment and allowing their opponents and the moderator to take control. Consistent focus demands an appreciation of the moment, and it matters whether the candidate looks focused.

Candidates should not slouch or appear sloppy. Even though voters say these things do not matter, they do. How candidates care for themselves is frequently interpreted as their attention to detail and how much they will care for others. Posture, grooming, and professionalism can often matter more than details the candidate provides.

Rule 11:
Every candidate has a weakness. Candidates must be prepared to attack their opponent's and respond to attacks on theirs.

President Reagan's comment about not making age an issue in the campaign was more than humorous—it was a preemptive defense against a perceived weakness. As noted at the start of this book, his line had been rehearsed, tested, and tweaked. Acknowledgment of this potential weakness was the vital first step.

President Reagan and his campaign team could have chosen to diminish its importance and ignore it, which would have been a mistake. Instead, they diminished its importance by preparing for and attacking it (with deft humor).

It is also crucial to prepare to attack the weakness of one's opponent. Candidates who are prepared to do so can deliver a brutal blow to their opponents.

Perhaps the best example of this occurred during a vice presidential debate in 1988, when Democratic vice presidential nominee, and then-Senator, Lloyd Bentsen delivered one of the most memorable zingers of any political debate ever. It is certainly one of the most quoted lines in the history of political debates.

At the time of the October 1988 debate taking place in Omaha, Nebraska, then-Senator Quayle was 41 years old, and his youth was being raised as a concern about whether he was experienced enough to be "the next in line to be president." He had taken up the habit on the campaign trail of comparing his experience to that of President John F. Kennedy before JFK had been elected to the highest office in the land (Quayle had twelve years of Congressional service, Kennedy had fourteen).

His perceived weakness (age) was the opposite end of the spectrum from that faced by President Reagan's and, like the outgoing incumbent, then-Senator Quayle was choosing to preemptively address it.

As Dukakis campaign adviser Susan Estrich tells the story, the Democratic vice presidential candidate was participating in practice debates (with Dennis Eckart playing the role of Senator Quayle), and Senator Bentsen was surprised to hear the stand-in use the line comparing his Senator Quayle to President Kennedy (see, practice debates matter!). His desire to reply to the comparison was affirmed by the campaign team and rehearsed in practice. The trap was set.

When Senator Quayle was pressed by the questioners as to his ability to serve as president should circumstances arise, the Indiana Senator repeated his stump speech lines and the Texas Senator pounced: "Senator, I served with Jack Kennedy. I knew Jack Kennedy. Jack Kennedy was a friend of mine. Senator, you're no Jack Kennedy."

The crowd erupted as the verbal dagger found its mark. The problem for Senator Bentsen was that, while his vice presidential opponent may have been "no Jack Kennedy," neither was his running mate (VP debates are, *at best*, the opening act).

Summary

Prepare with a plan. Practice to improve performance. Stay on message and maintain a positive and calm demeanor. These basics can be accomplished by even the least eloquent candidates.

For those candidates with rhetorical skills: practice attack lines and responses to lines of attack, especially those targeting perceived weaknesses; be confident enough to effectively deploy controlled anger when appropriate; never let the rules be an obstacle to emphasizing core messages, and be ready for moments when the tables can be turned and good defense can be replaced by great offense. And whatever happens, smile and talk about the color Red.

BIBLIOGRAPHY & ADDITIONAL REFERENCES

For a wealth of archived material, including transcripts of many debates, the website of The Commission on Presidential Debates (https://www.debates.org/) is an invaluable resource. Below are other scholarly and journalistic articles covering a wide variety of topics related to political debates, both domestic and international:

Birdsell, D. (2017). Political Campaign Debates. In *The Oxford Handbook of Political Communication*, eds. Kate Kenski and Kathleen Hall Jamieson. Oxford University Press.

Bond, G. D., Holman, R. D., Eggert, J. A. L., Speller, L. F., Garcia, O. N., Mejia, S. C., ... & Rustige, R. (2017). "Lyin" Ted", "Crooked Hillary", and "Deceptive Donald": Language of Lies in the 2016 US Presidential Debates. *Applied Cognitive Psychology*, 31(6), 668-677.

Bos, A.L., van Doorn B.W., Smanik, A.C. (2012). The Effects of HDTV on Perceptions of Obama and McCain in a 2008 Presidential Debate. *Communication Research Reports*, 29(2), 161-168.

Brands, H.W. (2011). Debates Are Slugfests That Promote Extremism. *The New York Times* (online), October 28, 2011. https://www.nytimes.com/roomfordebate/2011/10/23/do-good-debaters-make-good-presidents/debates-are-slugfests-that-promote-extremism

Browne, A. (2018). 8 of the Best Moments in Presidential Debates. *History Hit TV* (online), August 16, 2018. https://www.historyhit.com/best-moments-in-presidential-debates/

Cavgias, A., Corbi, R., Meloni, L., & Novaes, L. M. (2019). *Edited democracy: media manipulation and the news coverage of presidential debates* (No. 2019_17). University of São Paulo (FEA-USP). [analyzing Presidential Debates in Brazil]

Cho, J., Ha, Y. (2012). On the Communicative Underpinnings of Campaign Effects: Presidential Debates, Citizen Communication, and Polarization in Evaluations of Candidates. *Political Communication*, 2012(2), 184-204.

Dallek, R. (2011). Presidential Debates: To Spar Is Not To Govern. *The New York Times* (online), October 28, 2011. https://www.nytimes.com/roomfordebate/2011/10/23/do-good-debaters-make-good-presidents/presidential-debates-to-spar-is-not-to-govern

Echeverria, M. (2017). Journalistic infotainment in election coverage. The case of presidential debates. *Convergencia Revista de Ciencias Sociales*, 74, 1405-35. [analyzing Presidential debates in Mexico]

Estrich, S. (2004). The Debates. *NewsMax* (online), September 27, 2004. https://web.archive.org/web/20090510072124/http://archive.newsmax.com/archives/articles/2004/9/27/103737.shtml

Gergen, D. (2011). Rhetorical Skill Is Necessary, but Not Sufficient. *The New York Times* (online), October 28, 2011. https://www.nytimes.com/roomfordebate/2011/10/23/do-good-debaters-make-good-presidents/rhetorical-skill-is-necessary-but-not-sufficient

Hamby, A.L. (2011). Would Jefferson Make the Cut? *The New York Times* (online), October 28, 2011. https://www.nytimes.com/roomfordebate/2011/10/23/do-good-debaters-make-good-presidents/would-jefferson-make-the-cut

Haltiwanger, J. (2019). Presidential debates have always been political theater. Business Insider, September 12, 2019. https://www.businessinsider.com/presidential-debates-memorable-moments-political-theater-2019-9

Henderson, N-M. (2016). 8 unforgettable presidential debate blunders. *CNN* (online), September 26, 2016. https://www.cnn.com/2016/09/26/politics/presidential-debate-mistakes-history/index.html

Hoff, J. (2011). Nixon, King of the Town Hall. *The New York Times* (online), October 28, 2011. https://www.nytimes.com/roomfordebate/2011/10/23/do-good-debaters-make-good-presidents/nixon-king-of-the-town-hall

Holbrook, T. M. (1999). Political learning from presidential debates. *Political Behavior*, 21(1), 67-89.

Howard, A. (2016). 10 Presidential Debates That Actually Made an Impact. *NBC News* (online), September 25, 2016. https://www.nbcnews.com/storyline/2016-presidential-debates/10-presidential-debates-made-impact-n650741

Jamieson, K. H., & Birdsell, D. S. (1990). *Presidential debates: The challenge of creating an informed electorate*. Oxford University Press on Demand.

Jamieson, K.H. (2011). In presidential debates, Personality Is Revealed. *The New York Times* (online), October 28, 2011. https://www.nytimes.com/roomfordebate/2011/10/23/do-good-debaters-make-good-presidents/in-presidential-debates-personality-is-revealed

Kane, P. (2020). As pandemic limits scrutiny, GOP fears lesser-known Democratic candidates will steamroll to Senate majority. *The Washington Post* (online), July 25, 2020. https://www.washingtonpost.com/powerpost/as-pandemic-limits-scrutiny-gop-fears-lesser-known-democratic-candidates-will-steamroll-to-senate-majority/2020/07/24/e7087534-cde3-11ea-b0e3-d55bda07d66a_story.html?hpid=hp_hp-banner-main_pkcapitol-535pm%3Ahomepage%2Fstory-ans.

Kraus, S. (2013). *Televised presidential debates and Public Policy*. Routledge.

Kraus, S. (1962). *The great debates: Kennedy vs. Nixon*. Indiana University Press.

Meacham, J. (2011). A Sense of Who They Are. *The New York Times* (online), October 28, 2011. https://www.nytimes.com/roomfordebate/2011/10/23/do-good-debaters-make-good-presidents/a-sense-of-who-they-are.

Mitchell, D. (2015). 10 Memorable Moments in Presidential Debate History. *Time* (online), September 16, 2015. https://time.com/4036109/memorable-moments-presidential-debates/

Nader, R. (2016). Interview with Amy Goodman of *Democracy Now*, as published online on May 10, 2016. Nader: The U.S. Political & Media System Is Designed to Obstruct, Silence Third-Party Candidates, May 10, 2016. https://www.democracynow.org/2016/5/10/nader_the_us_political_media_system

NCC (2016). 10 Famous Political Debate Moments. *National Constitution Center* (online), September 26, 2016. https://constitutioncenter.org/blog/10-famous-political-debate-moments/.

Ordway, D-M, and Wihbey, J. (2016). presidential debates and their effects: Research roundup. *Journalist's Resource*, September 20, 2016. Shorenstein Center on Media, Politics, and Public Policy. https://journalistsresource.org/studies/politics/elections/presidential-debates-effects-research-roundup/

Rogin, J. (2012). Obama did call Benghazi attack an "act of terror" - in Colorado. Foreign Policy; The Cable, October 16, 2012. https://foreignpolicy.com/2012/10/16/obama-did-call-benghazi-attack-an-act-of-terror-in-colorado/

Reeves, R. (2011). Why Debates Matter: Voting Is an Emotional Act. *The New York Times* (online), October 28, 2011. https://www.nytimes.com/roomfordebate/2011/10/23/do-good-debaters-make-good-presidents/why-debates-matter-voting-is-an-emotional-act.

Rzepecka, M. (2016). Analyzing televised presidential general election debates. Ad Americam. Journal of American Studies, (17), 197-209.

Schroeder, A. (2008). *Presidential debates: fifty years of high-risk TV*. Columbia University Press.

Shah, D. V., Hanna, A., Bucy, E. P., Lassen, D. S., Van Thomme, J., Bialik, K., ... & Pevehouse, J. C. (2016). Dual screening during presidential debates: Political nonverbals and the volume and valence of online expression. American Behavioral Scientist, 60(14), 1816-1843.

Sorace, S. (2019). Top 9 presidential primary debate moments in US history. *Fox News* (online), June 26, 2019. https://www.foxnews.com/politics/presidential-primary-debates-memorable-moments-us-history

Stewart, J. A. (2018). In Through the Out Door: Examining the Use of Outsider Appeals in Presidential Debates. *Presidential Studies Quarterly*, 48(1), 93-109.

Tan, C., Peng, H., & Smith, N. A. (2018, April). *"You are no Jack Kennedy": On Media Selection of Highlights from Presidential Debates*. In Proceedings of the 2018 World Wide Web Conference, pp. 945-954.

The Guardian (2016). Trump "prowls" behind Clinton during presidential debate - video. *The Guardian* (online), October 10, 2016. https://www.theguardian.com/us-news/video/2016/oct/10/donald-trump-behind-hillary-clinton-debate-video

ABOUT THE AUTHORS

RANDY EVANS debated for the University of West Georgia from 1976-80. During that time, his team won various intercollegiate debate tournaments. He then went on to work in various capacities preparing candidates from school board to President for political debates. His relationship with Speaker Gingrich spans over four decades.

Dr. Michael Hester, whose Ph.D. in Communications focused on Presidential Rhetoric, has been the Director of Debate at the University of West Georgia since 1995. In addition to being a three-time national championship coach and two-time

national coach of the year, he has extensive international education experience, teaching debate in East Asia, East Africa, and the Caribbean.

www.WinningPoliticalDebates.com